This book belongs to:

....

....

Join the **Emu North** family!

We're building a vibrant, **supportive space** for all things colouring.

Drop in, say hello, let's **share the fun** and our creative journeys!

@emunorth

emunorth.com

© Emu North 2025, all rights reserved

If using wet pens, place a blank piece of paper behind the page

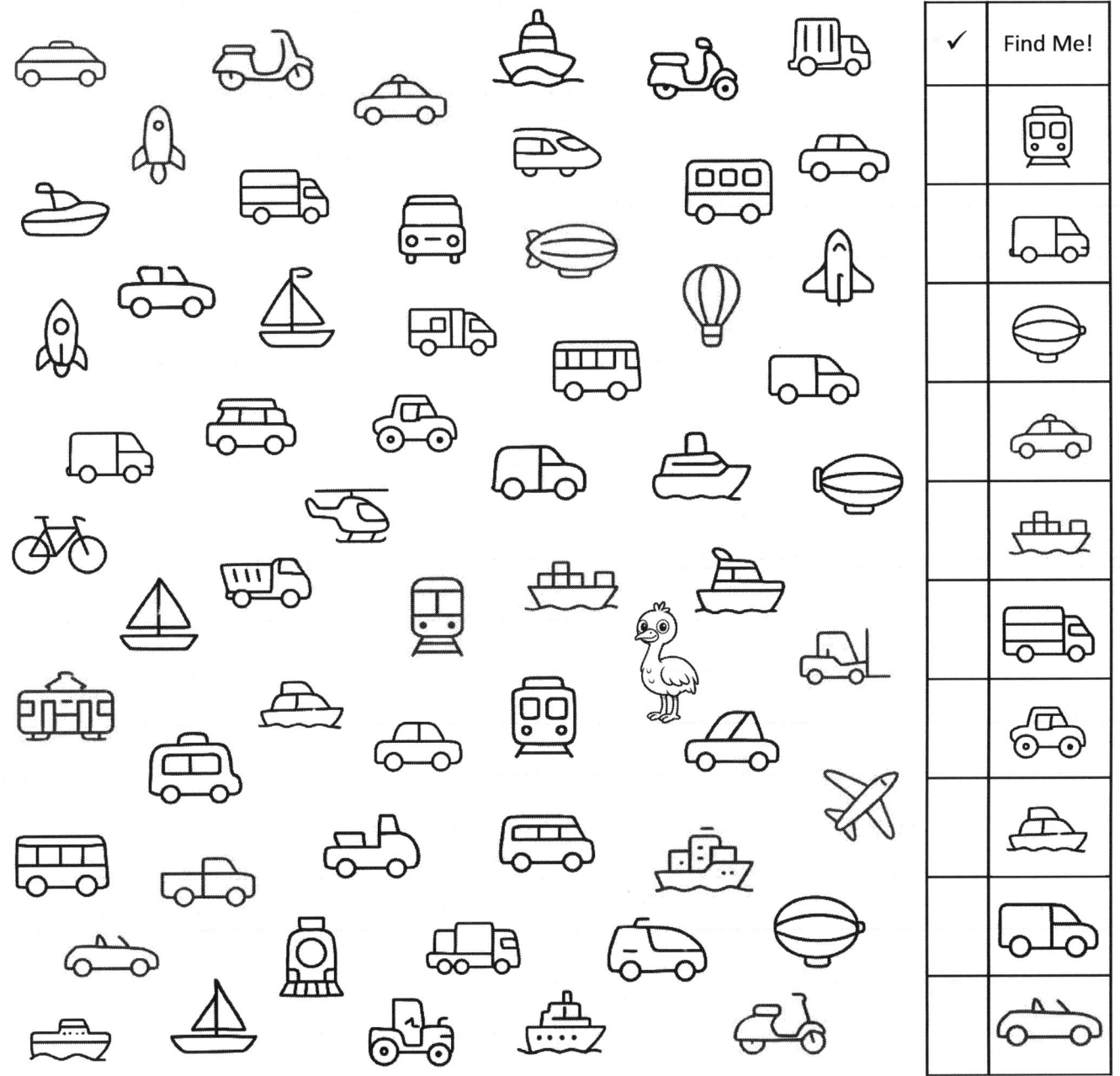

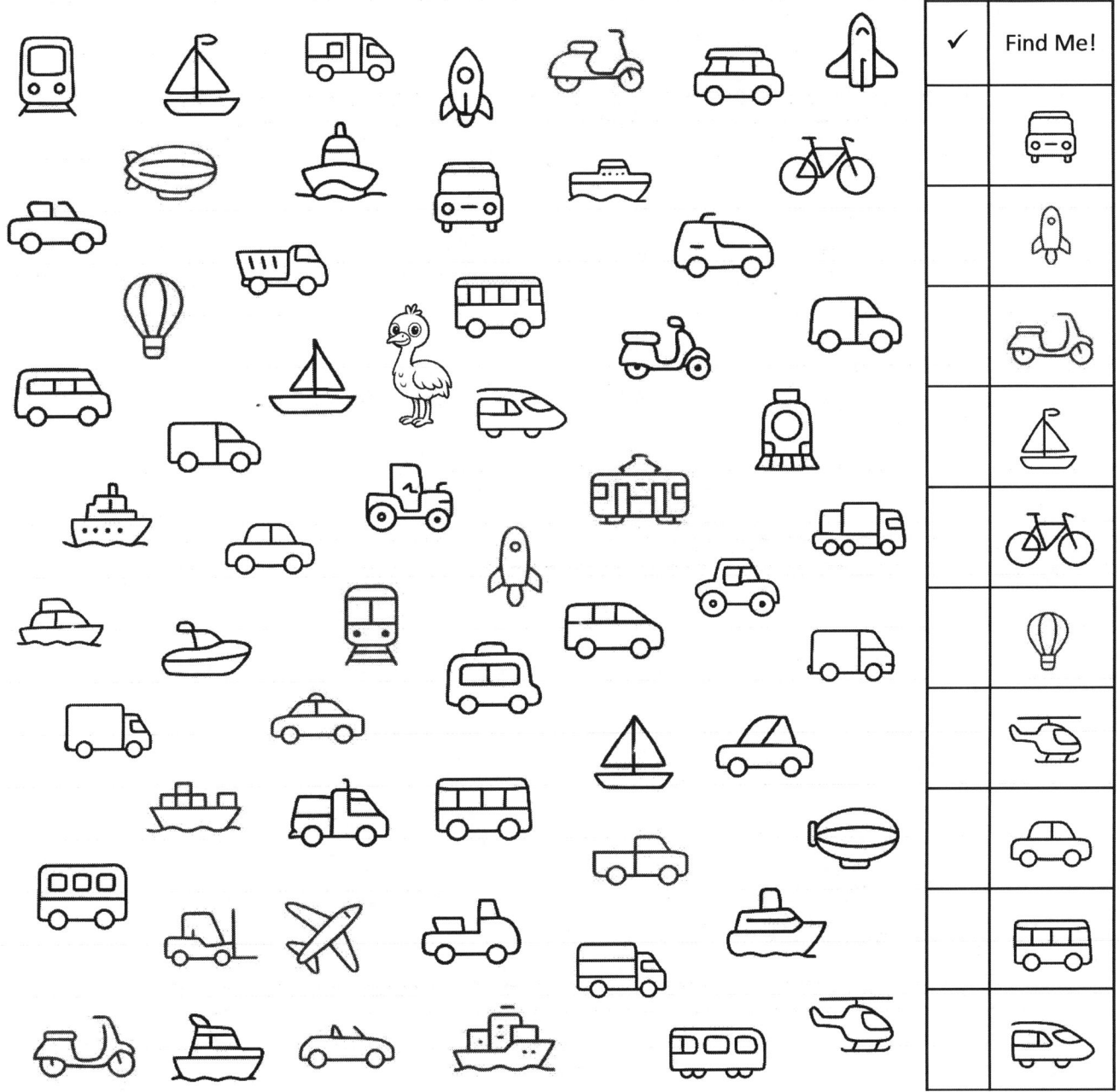

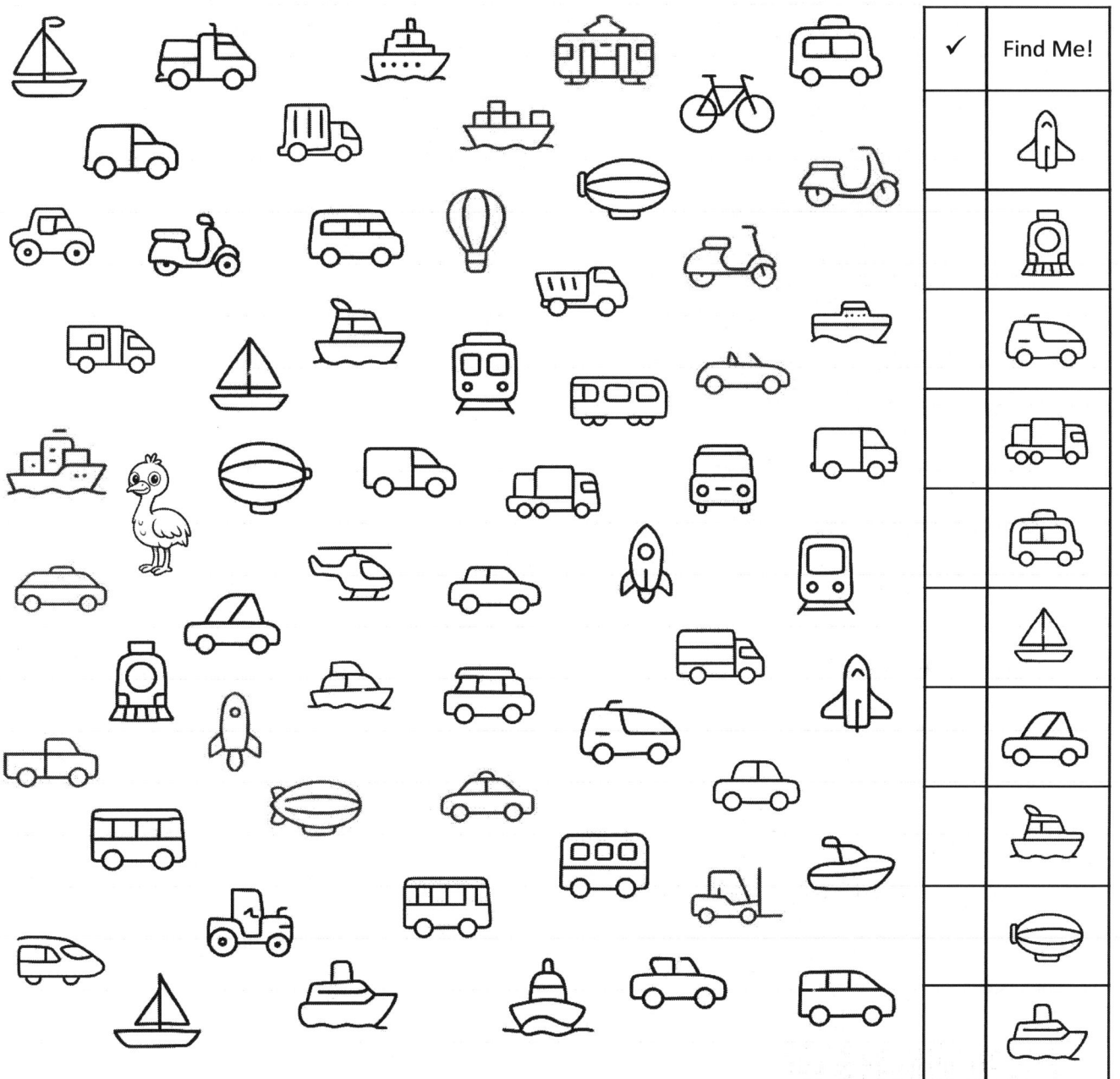

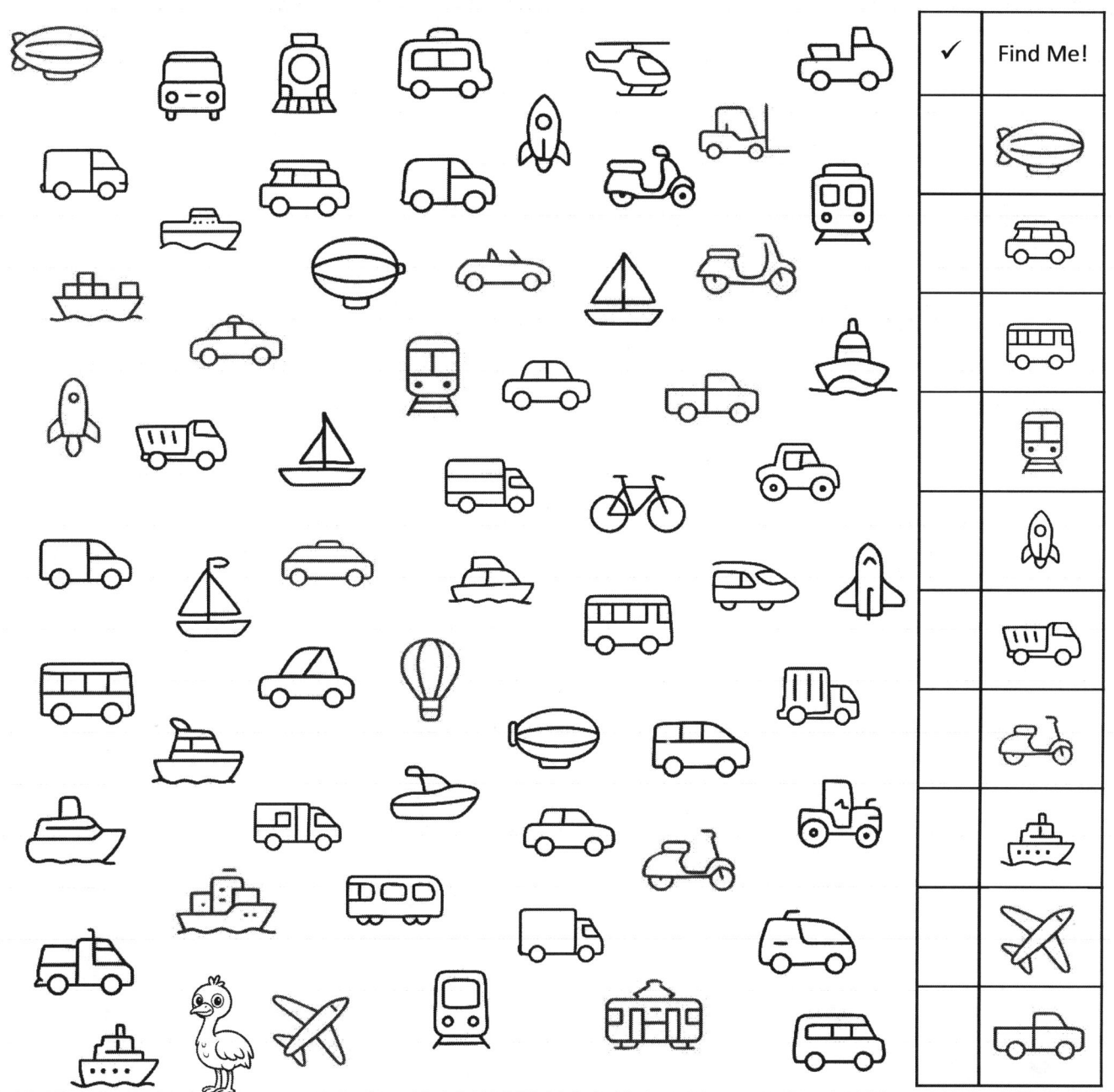

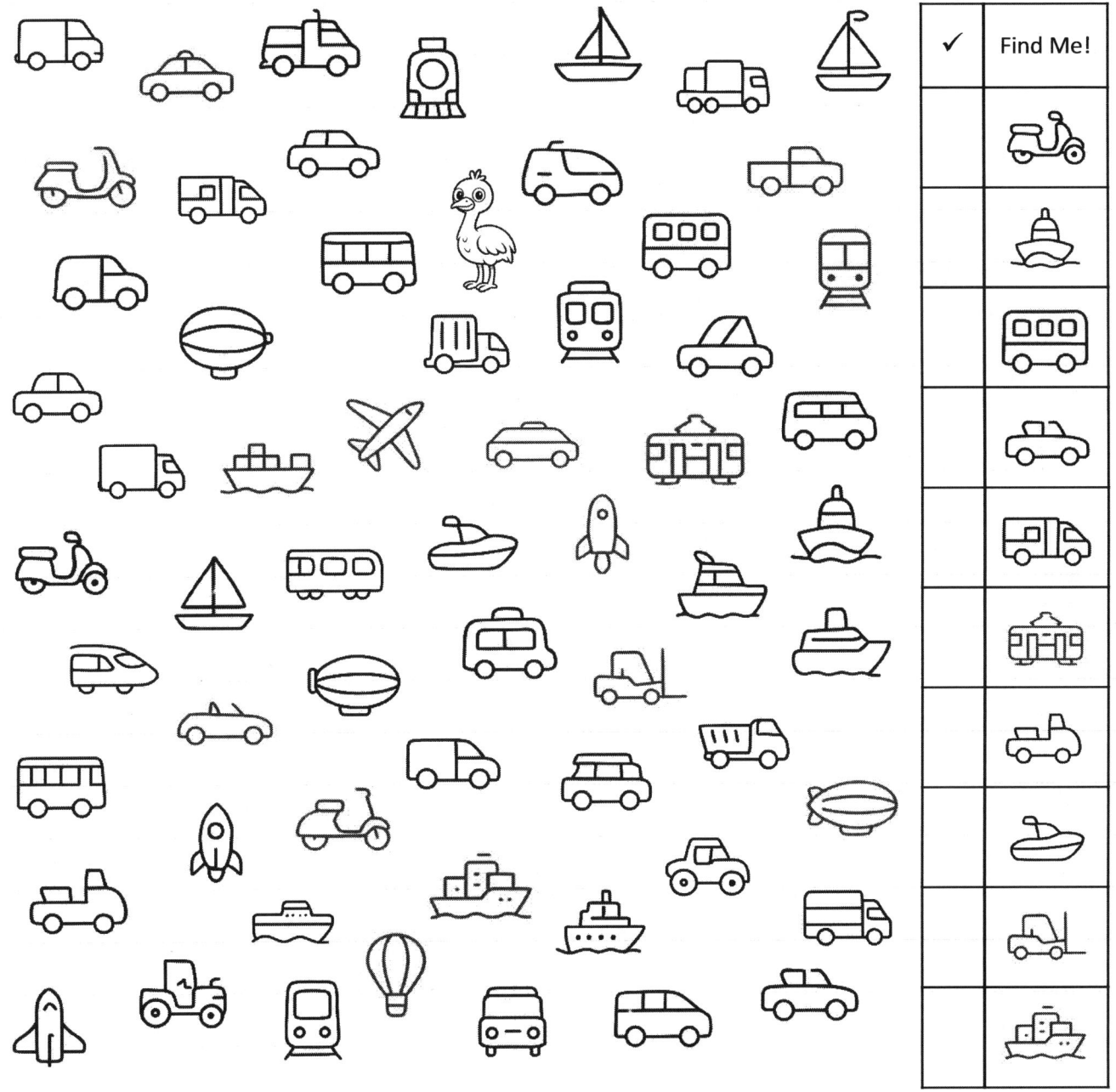

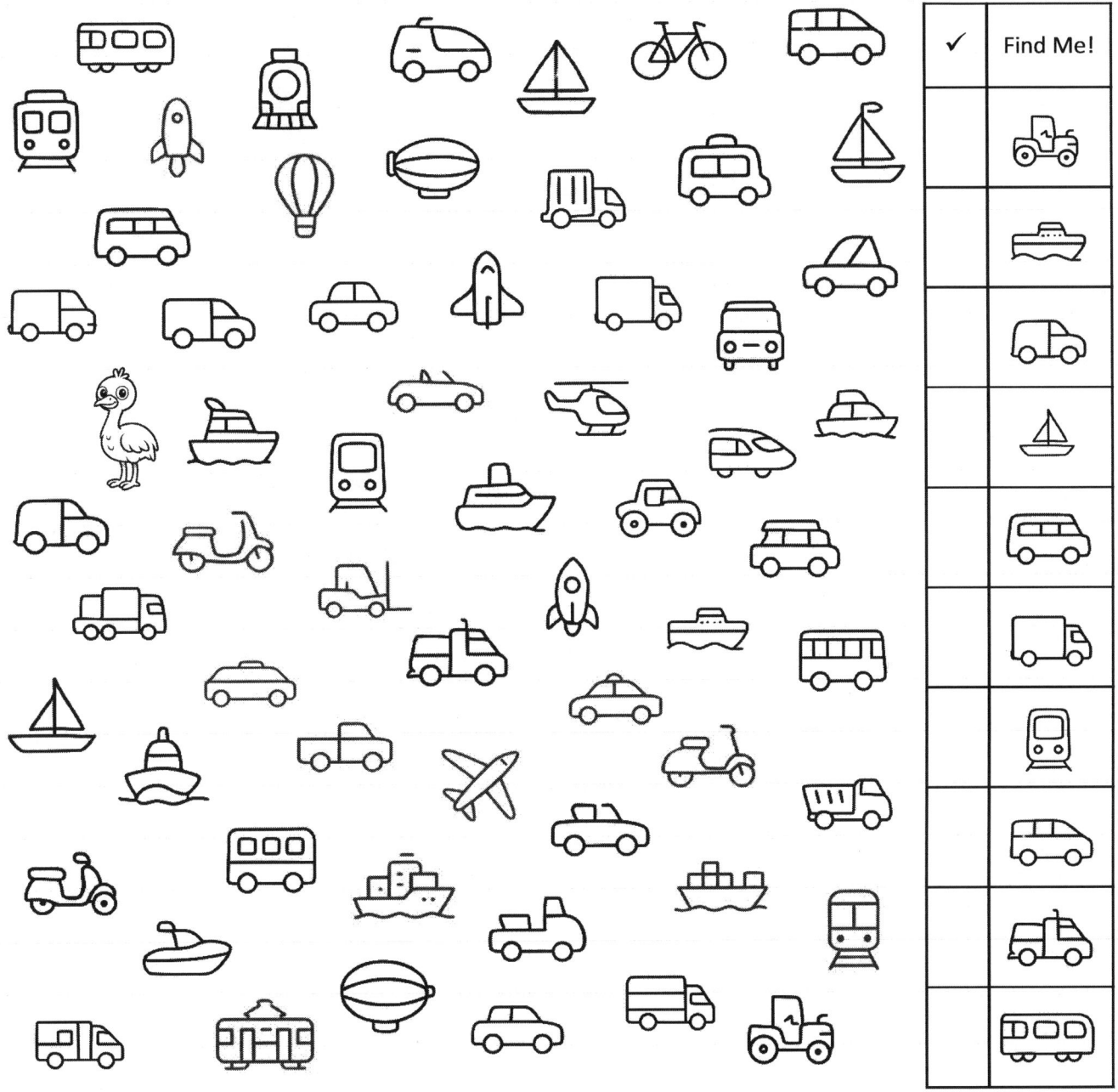

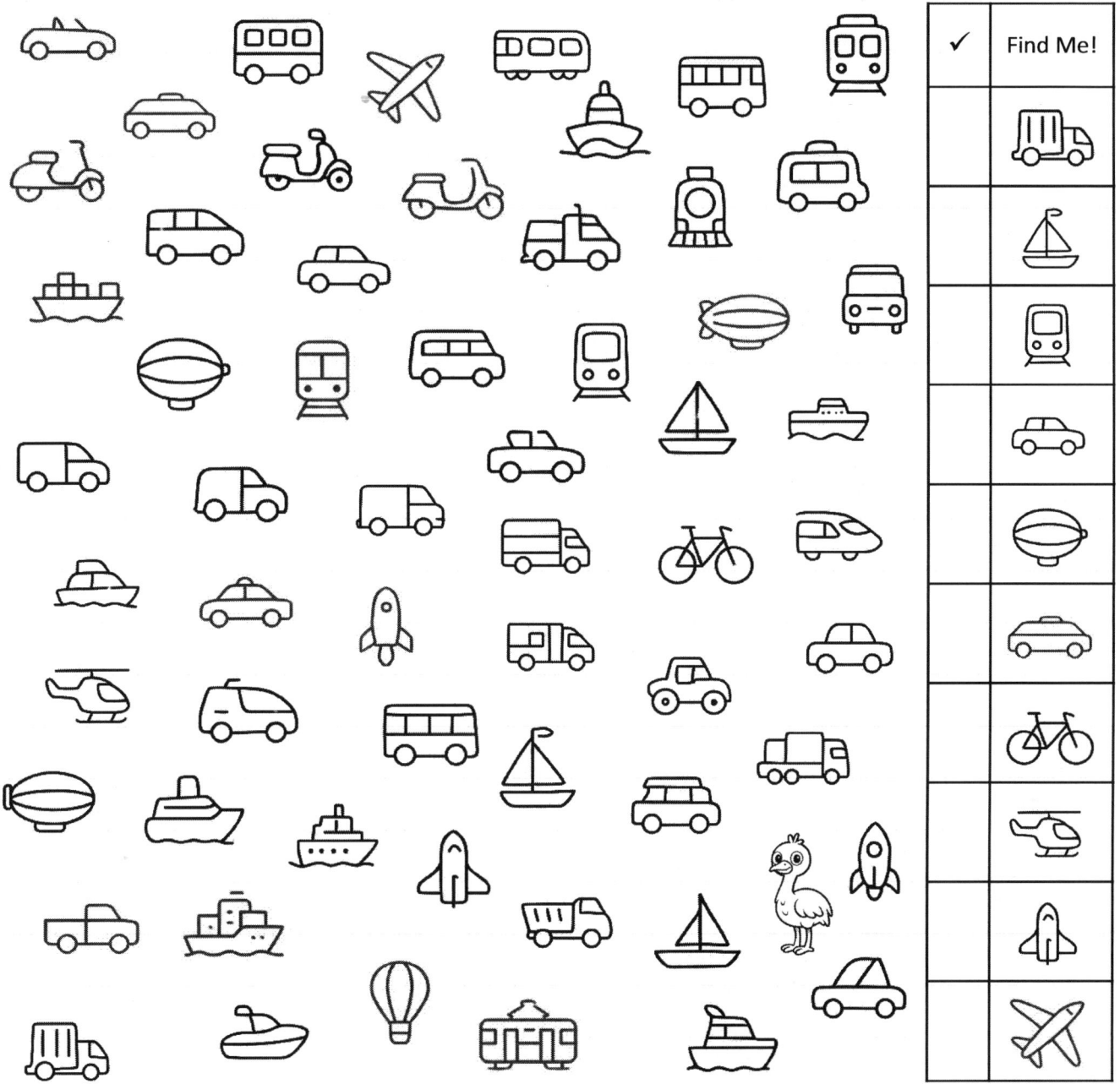

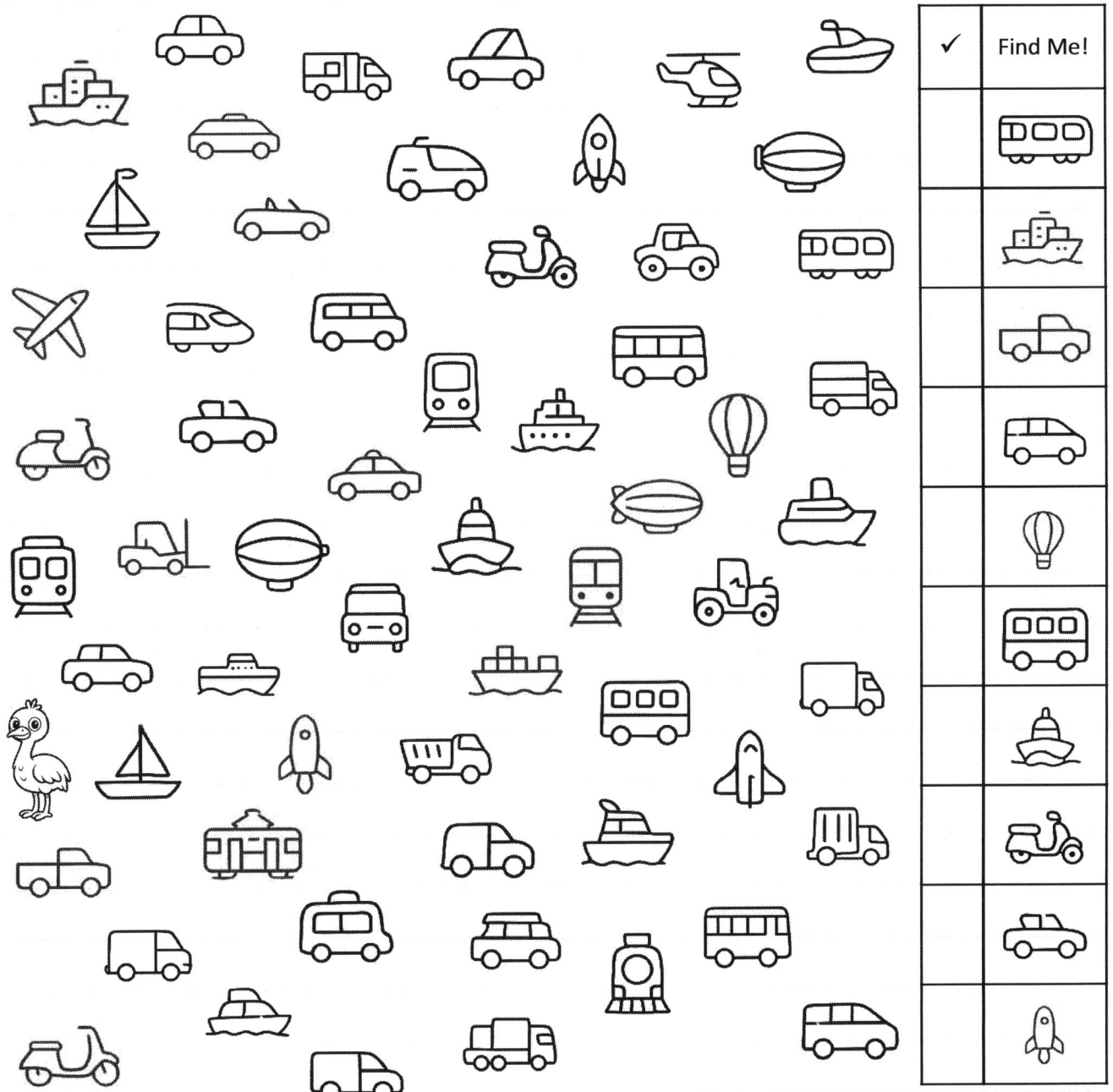

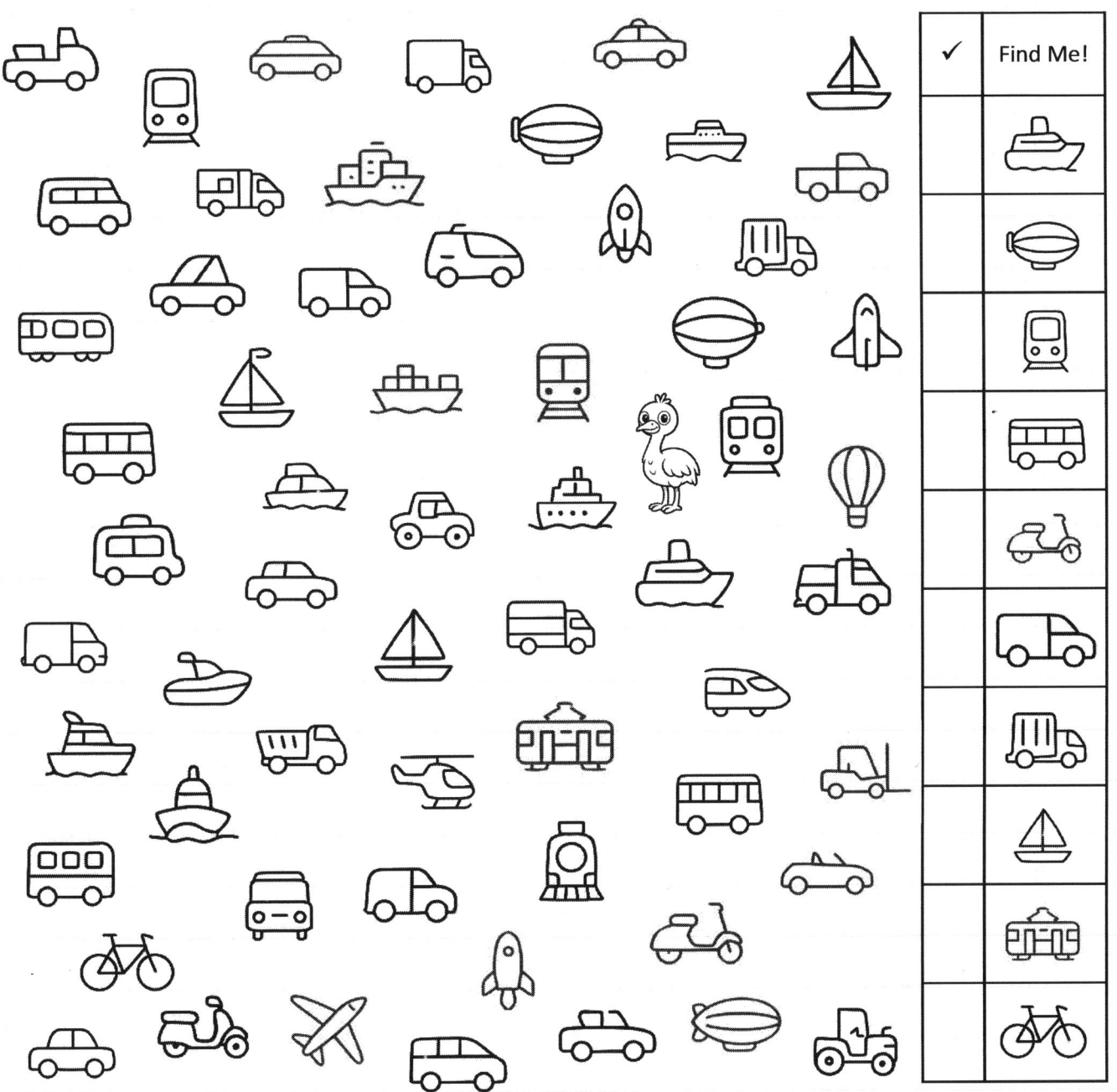

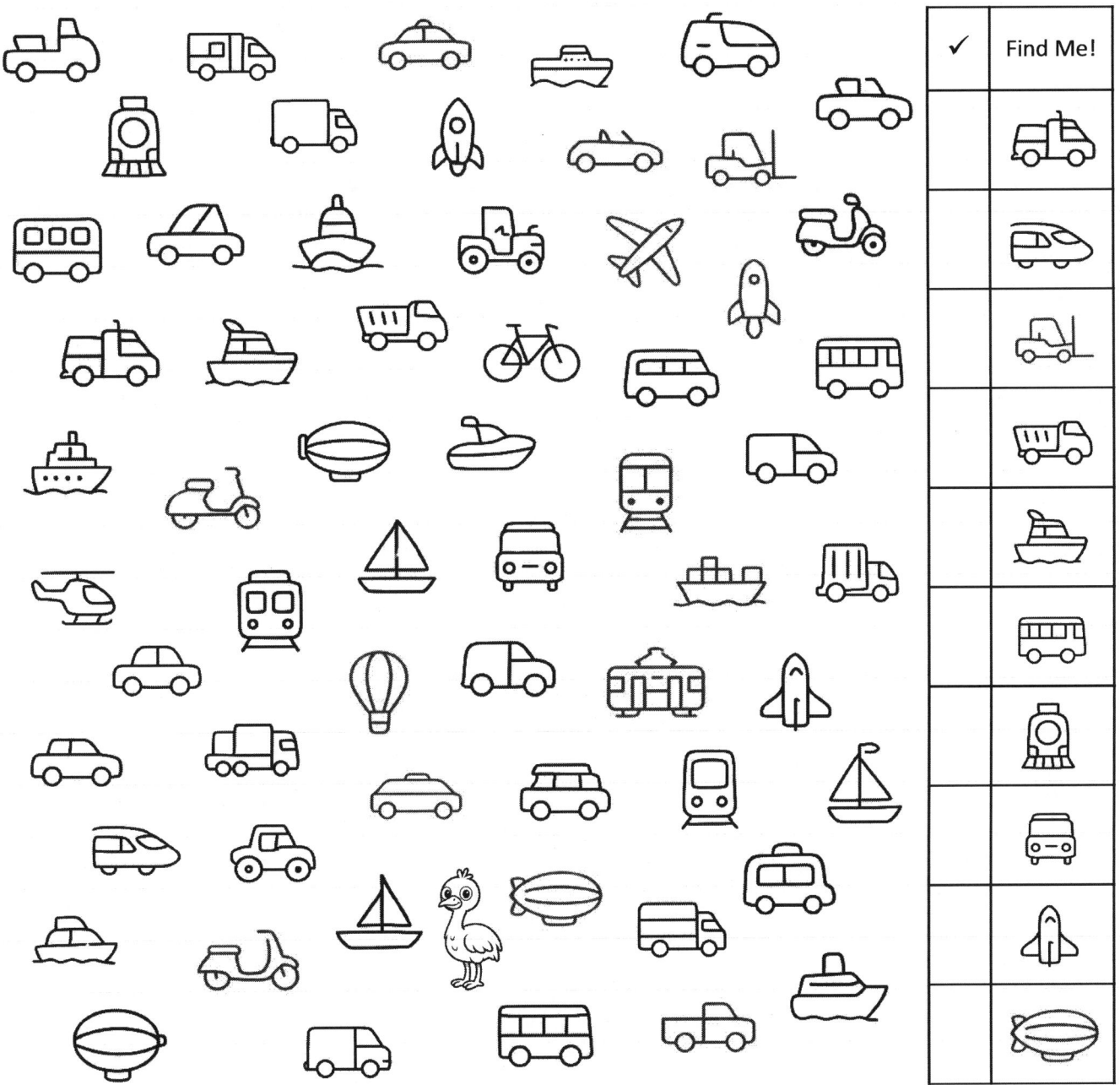

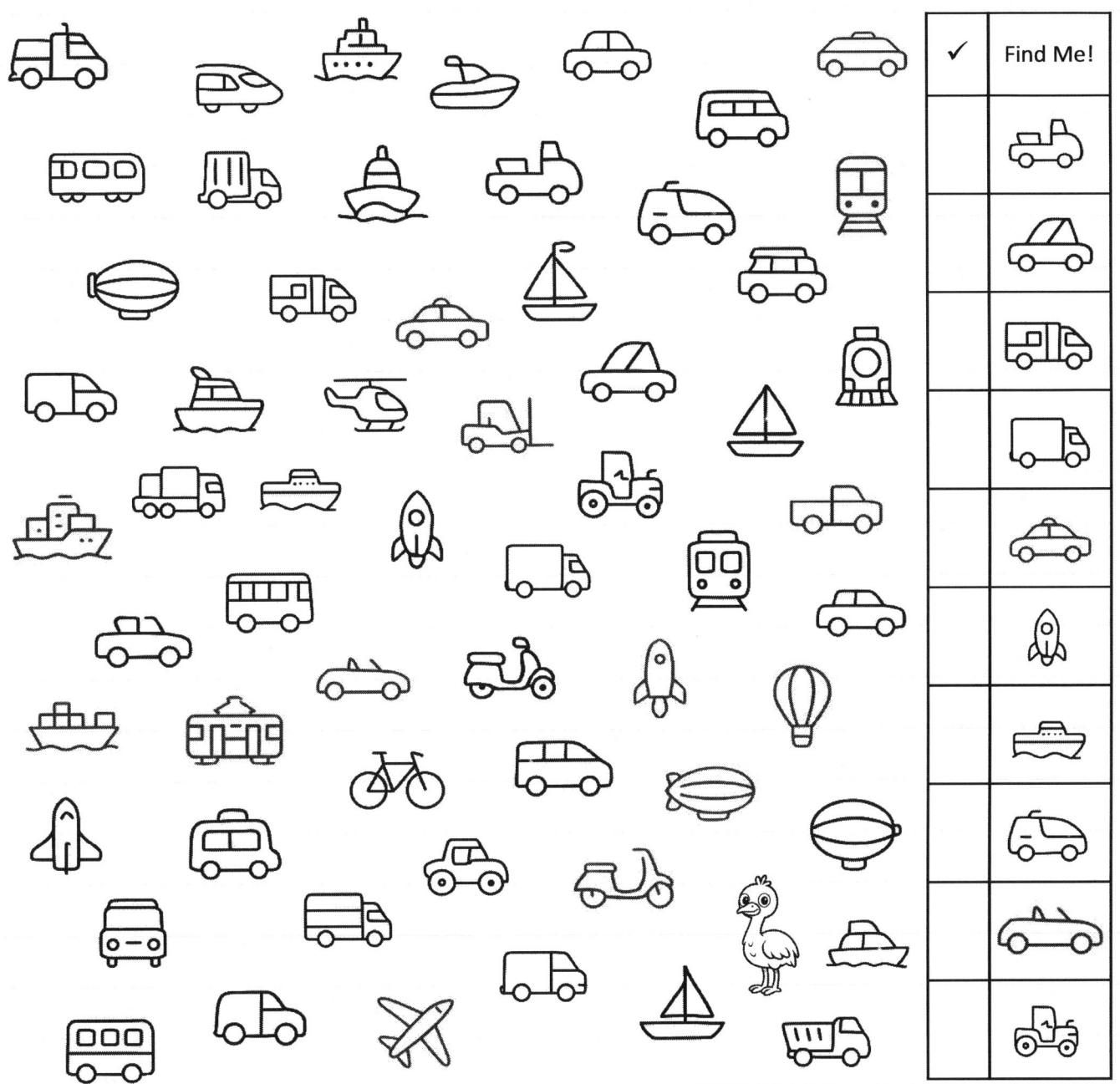

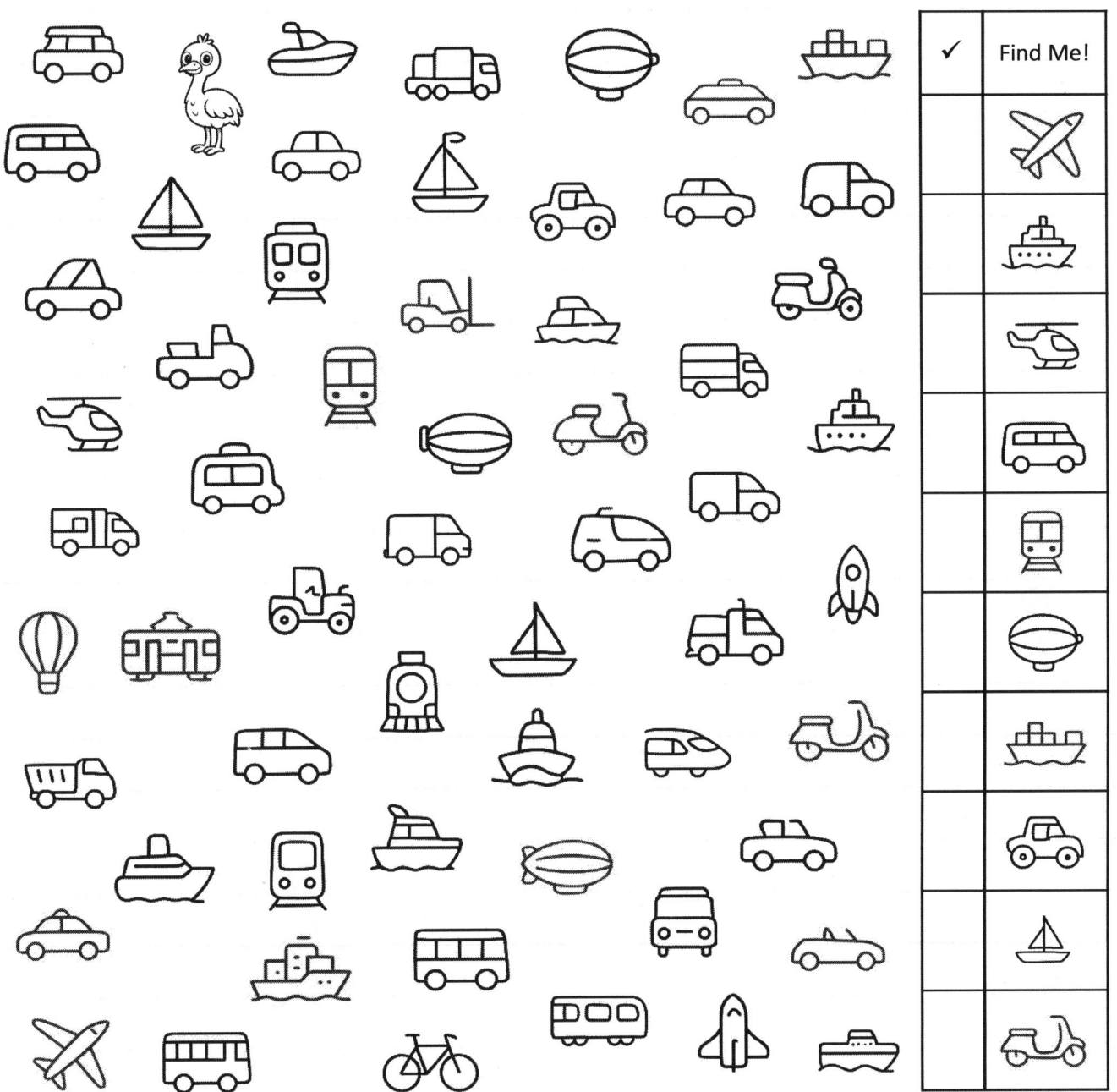

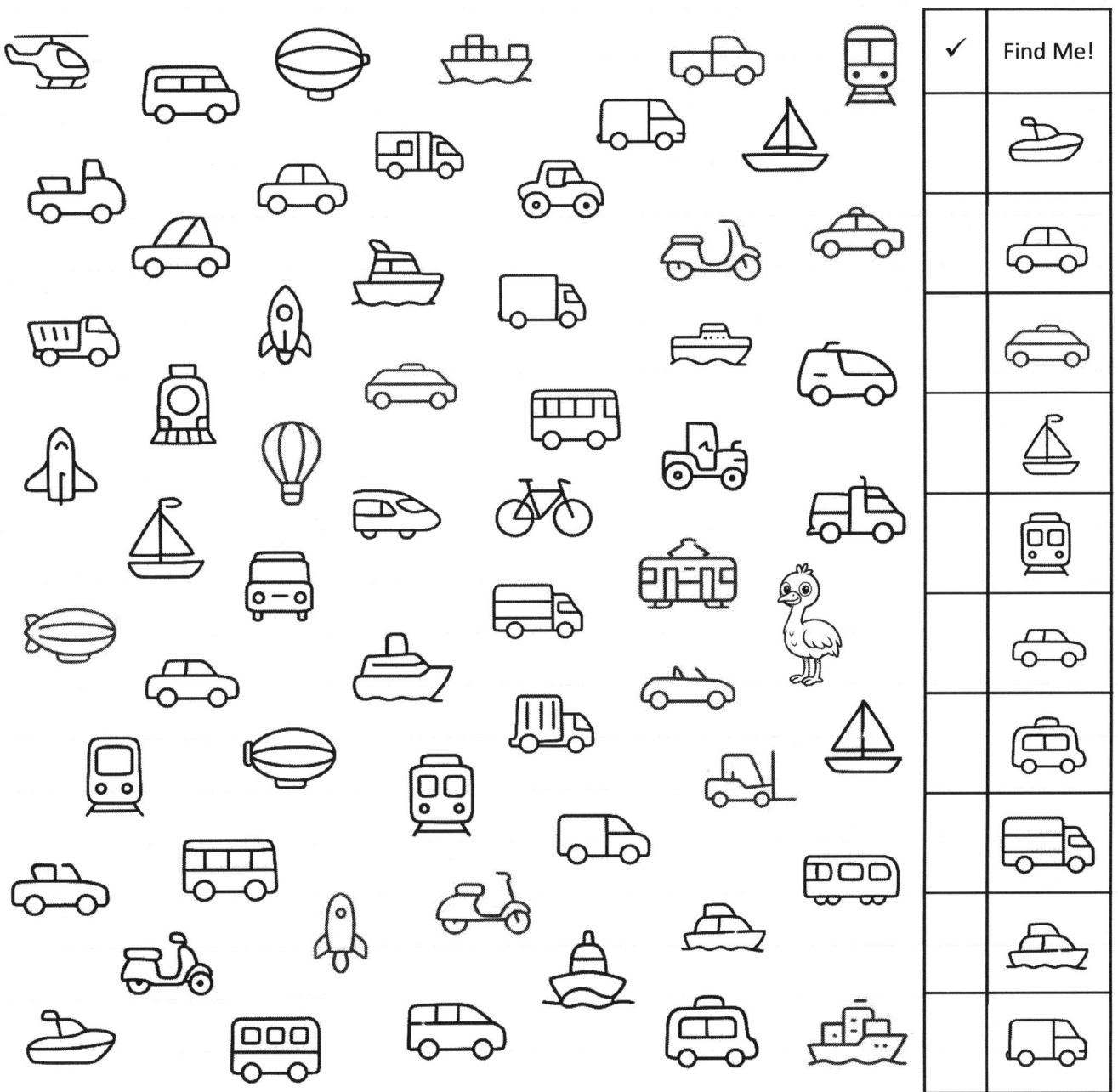

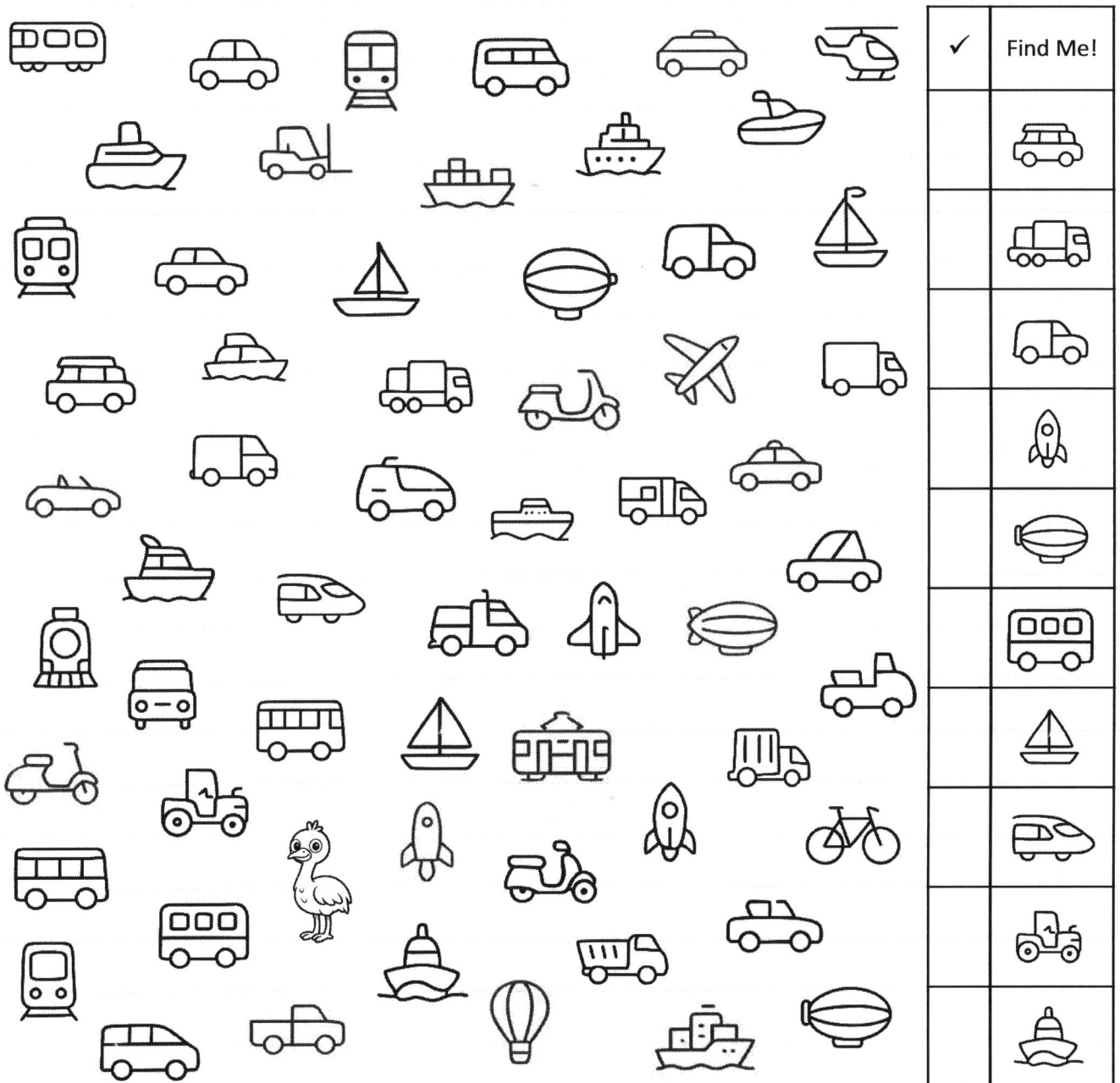

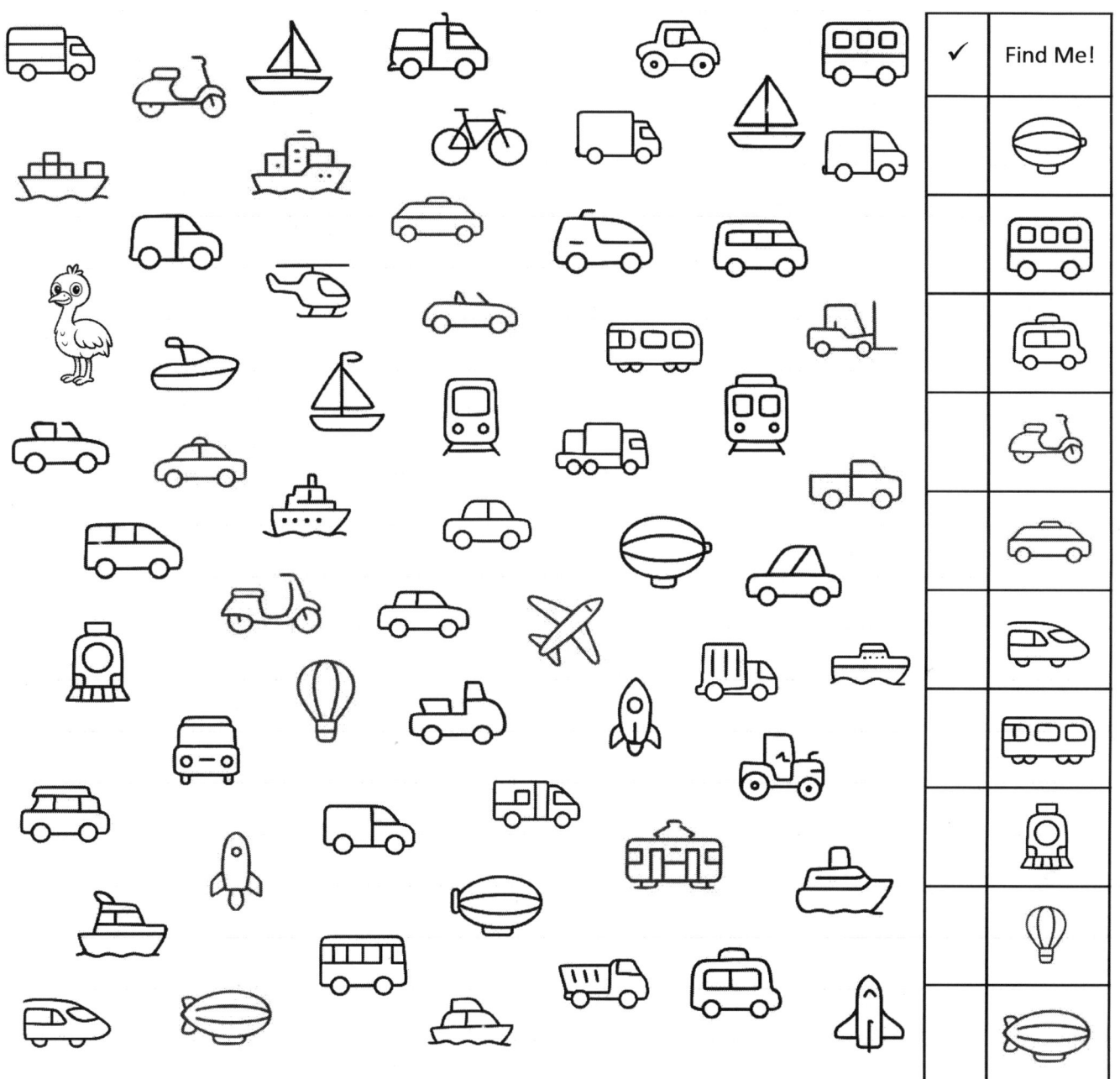

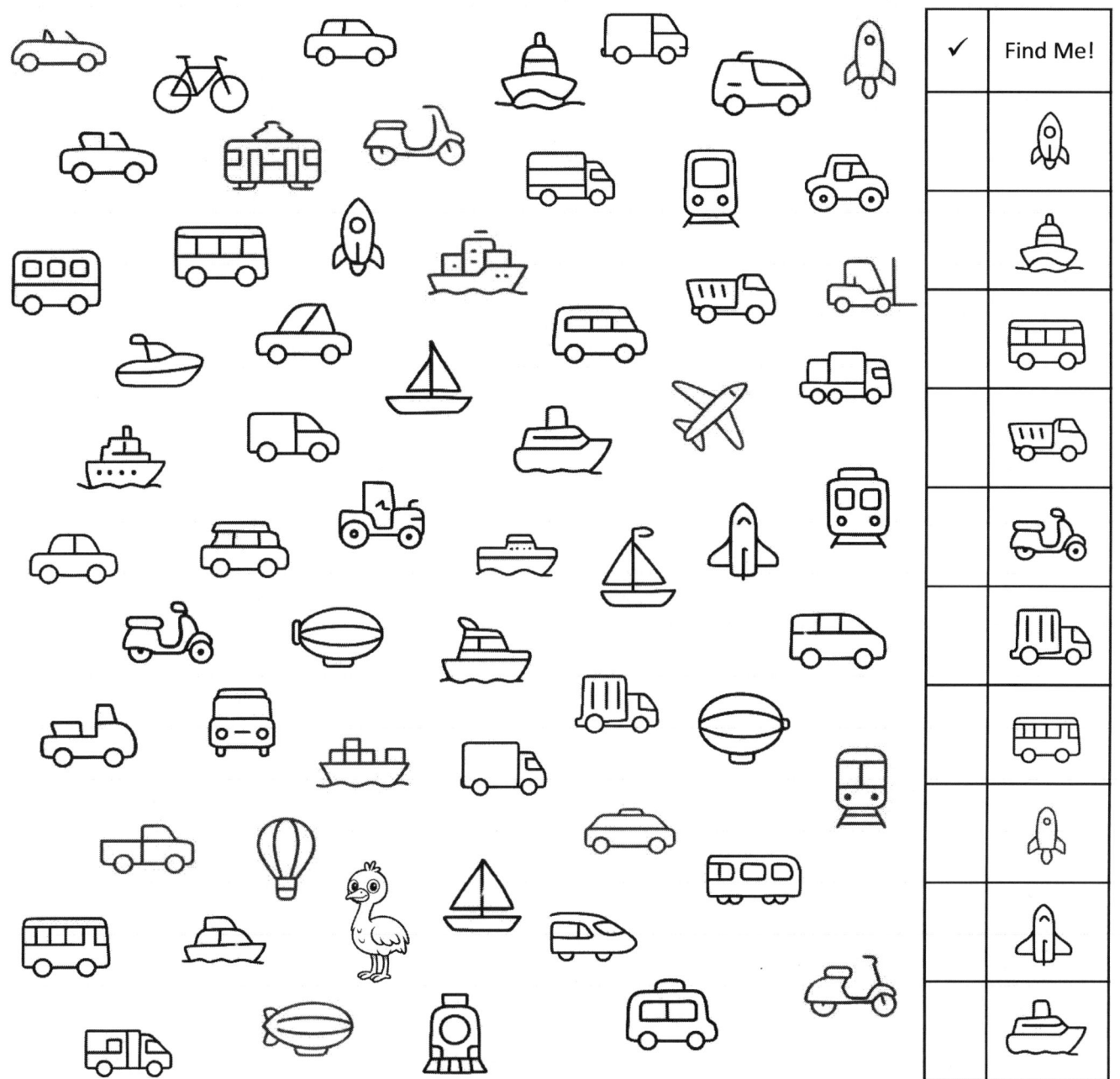

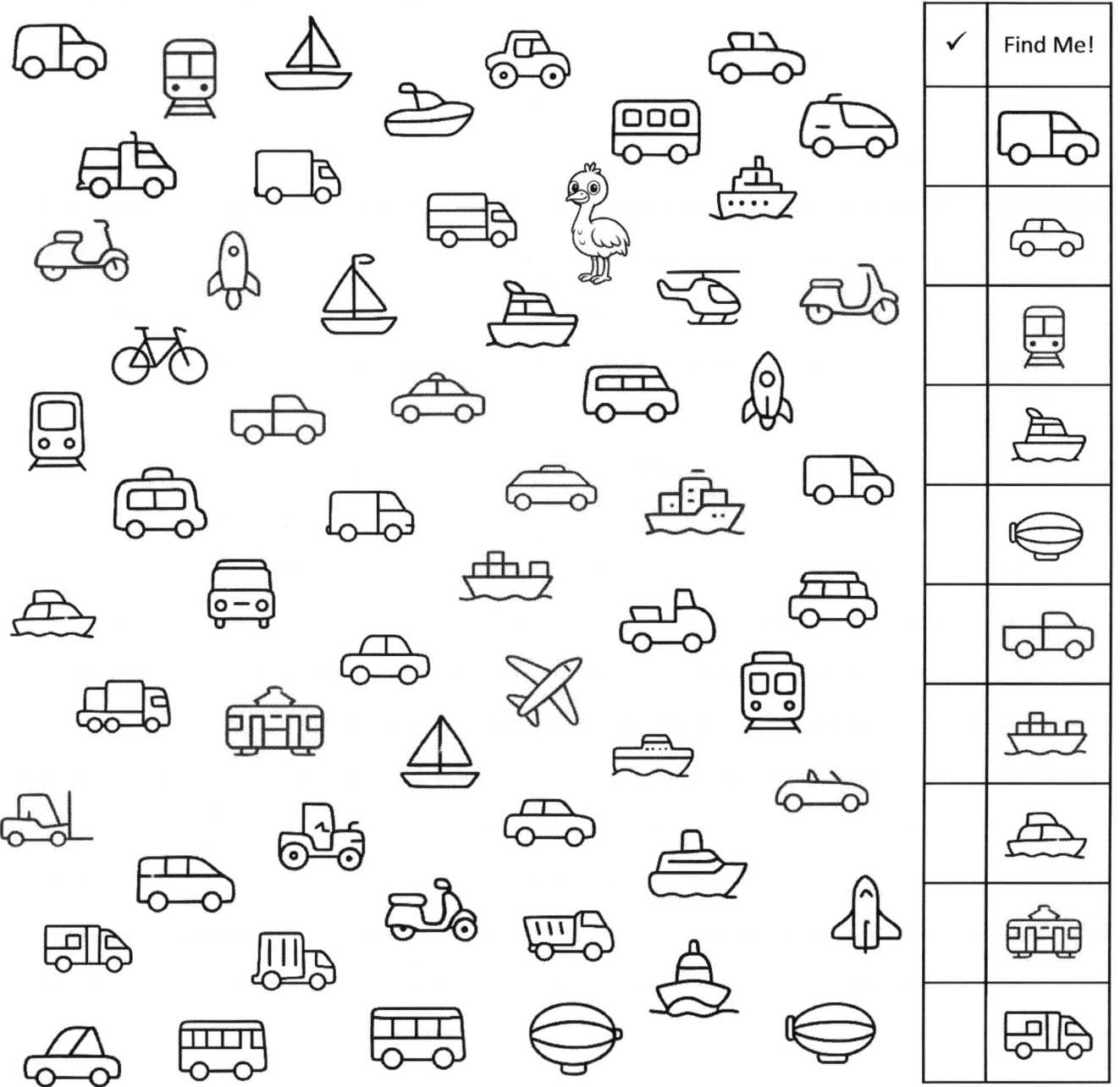

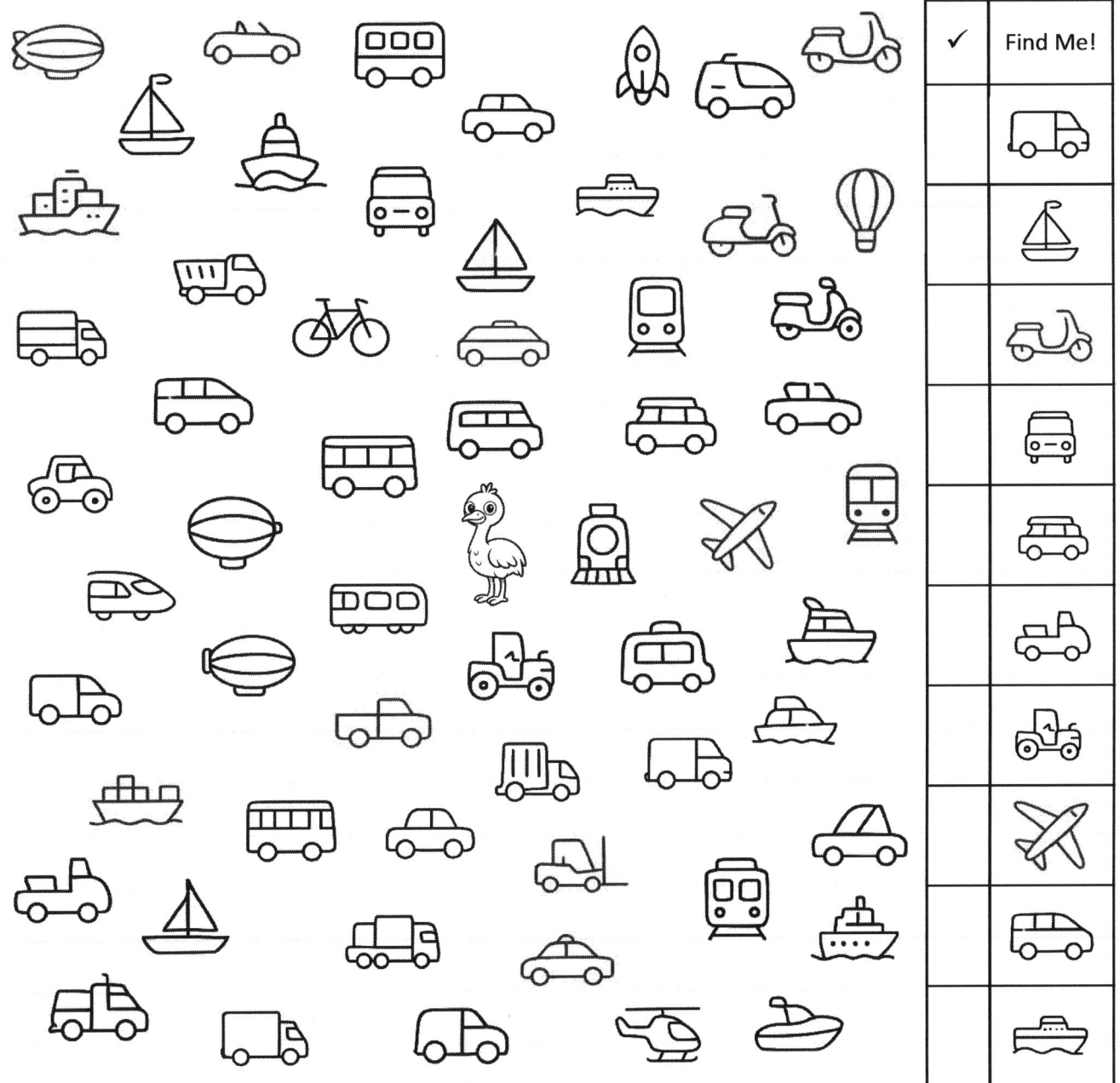

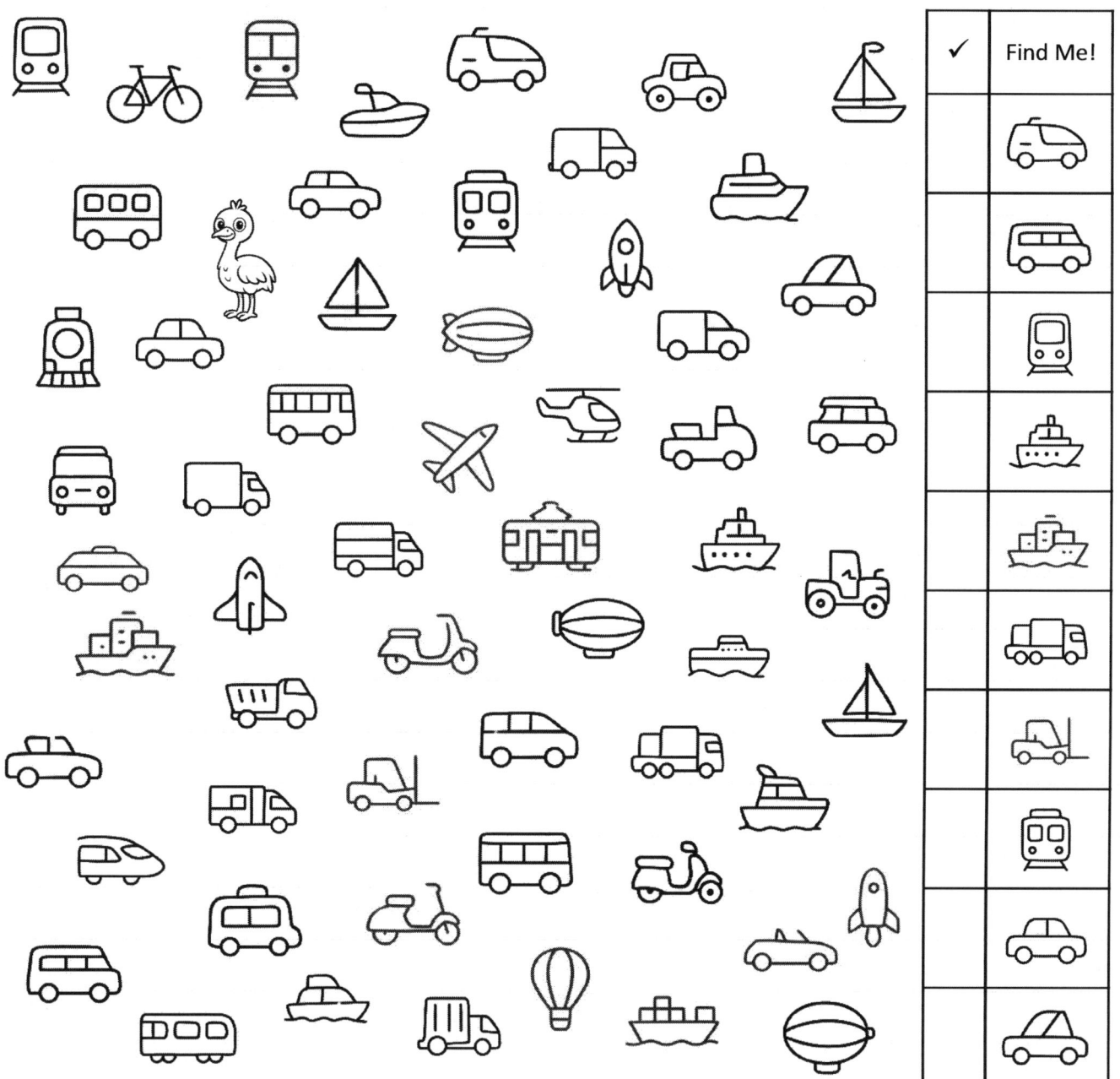

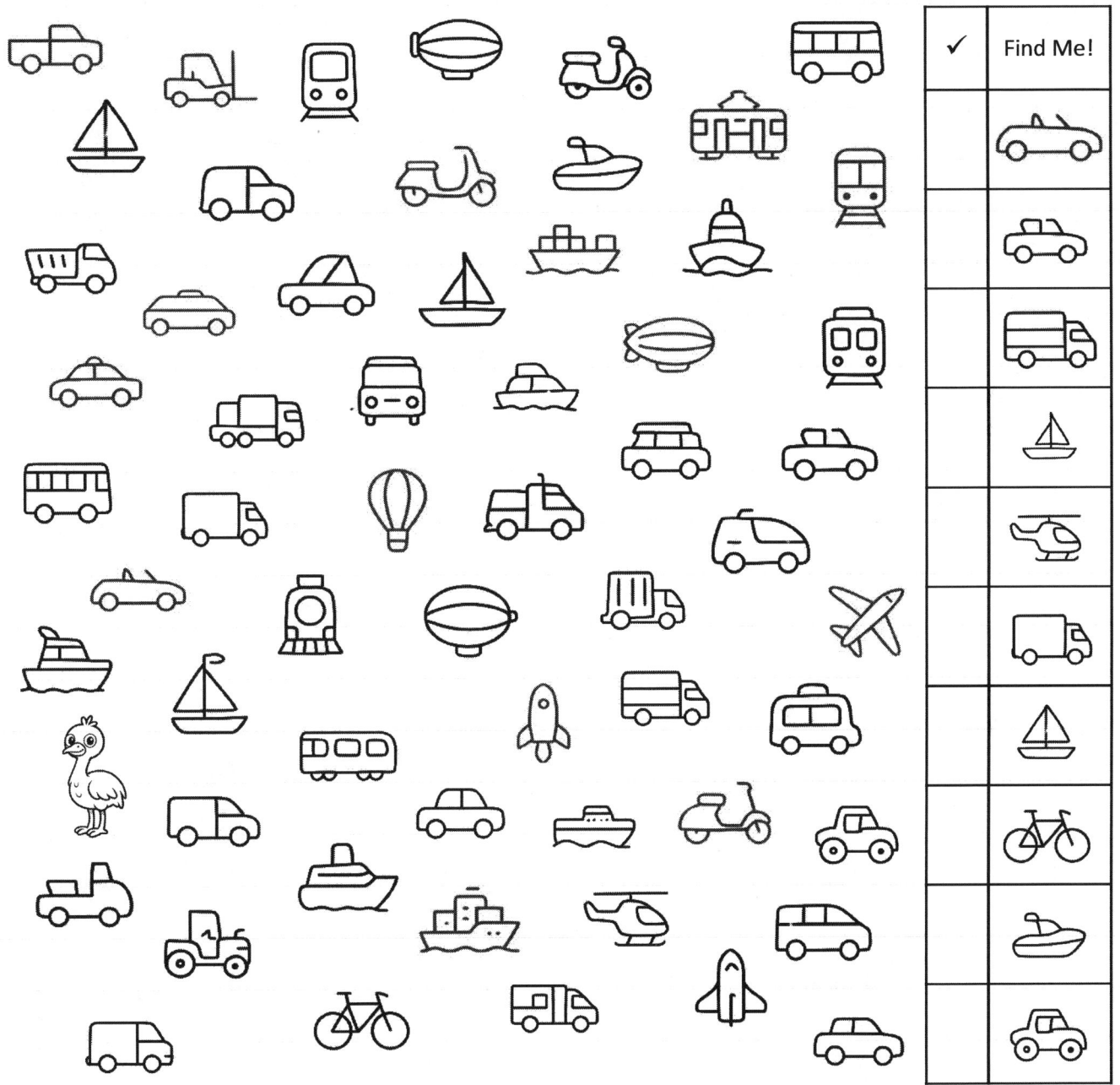

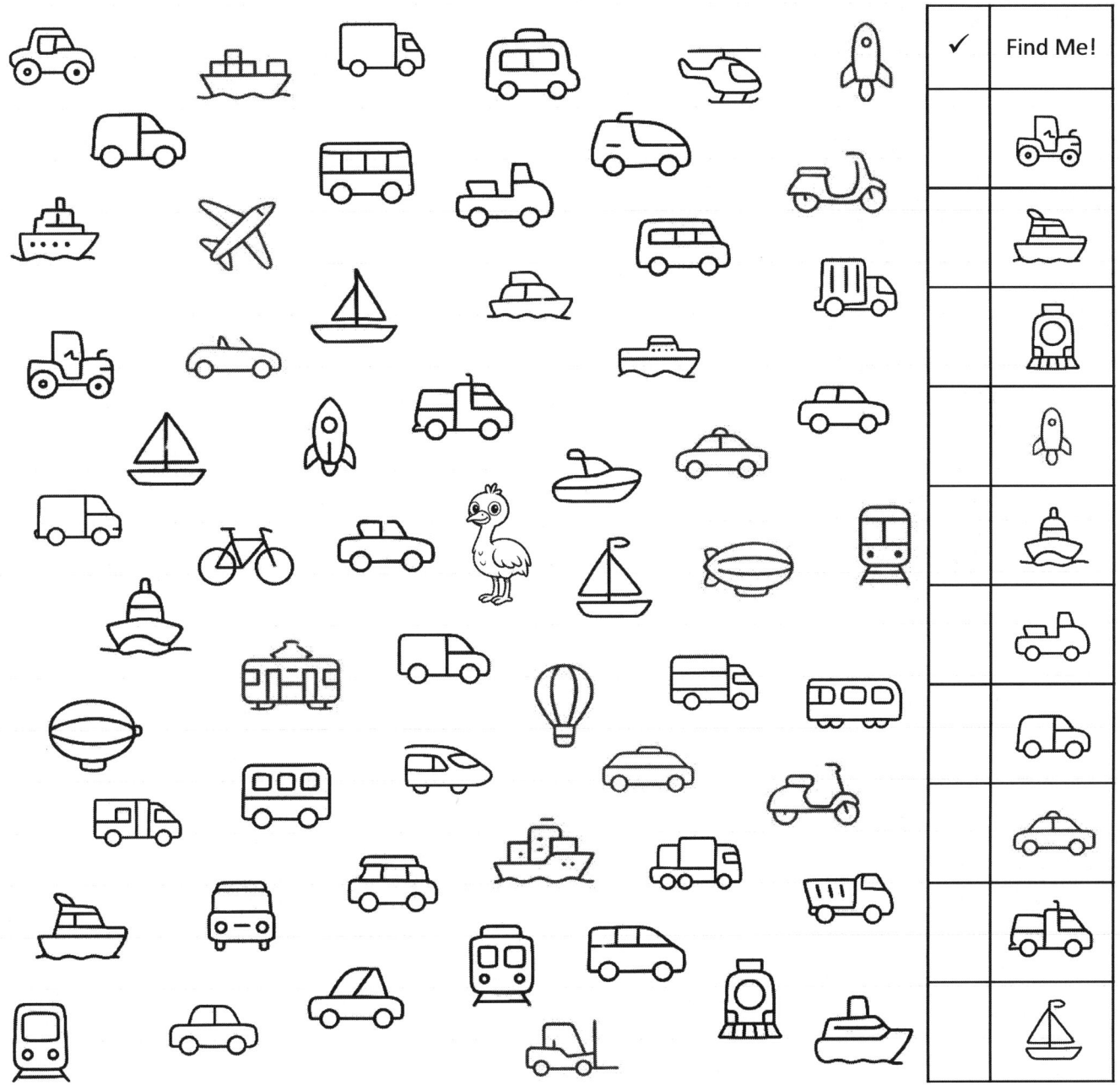

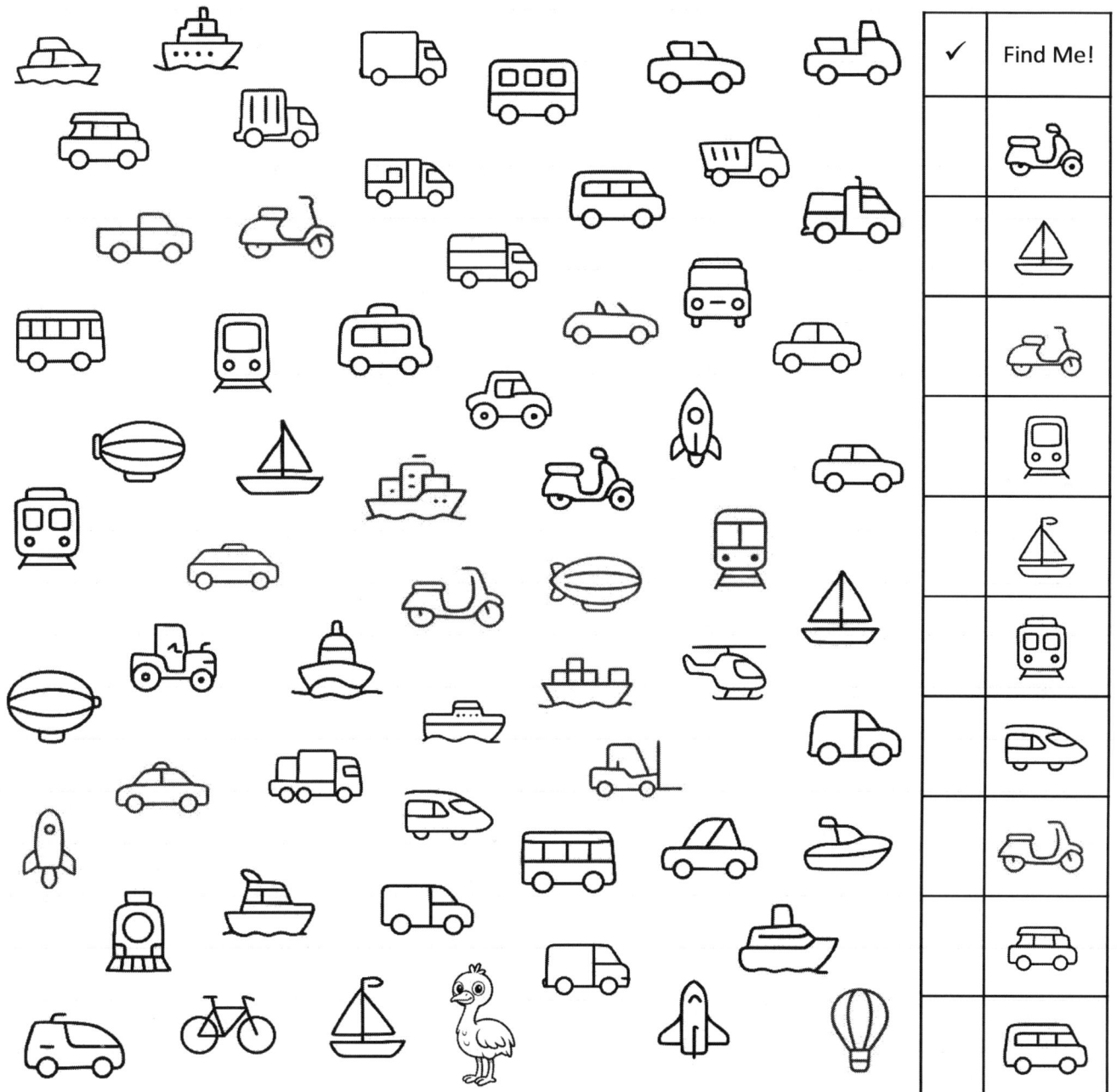

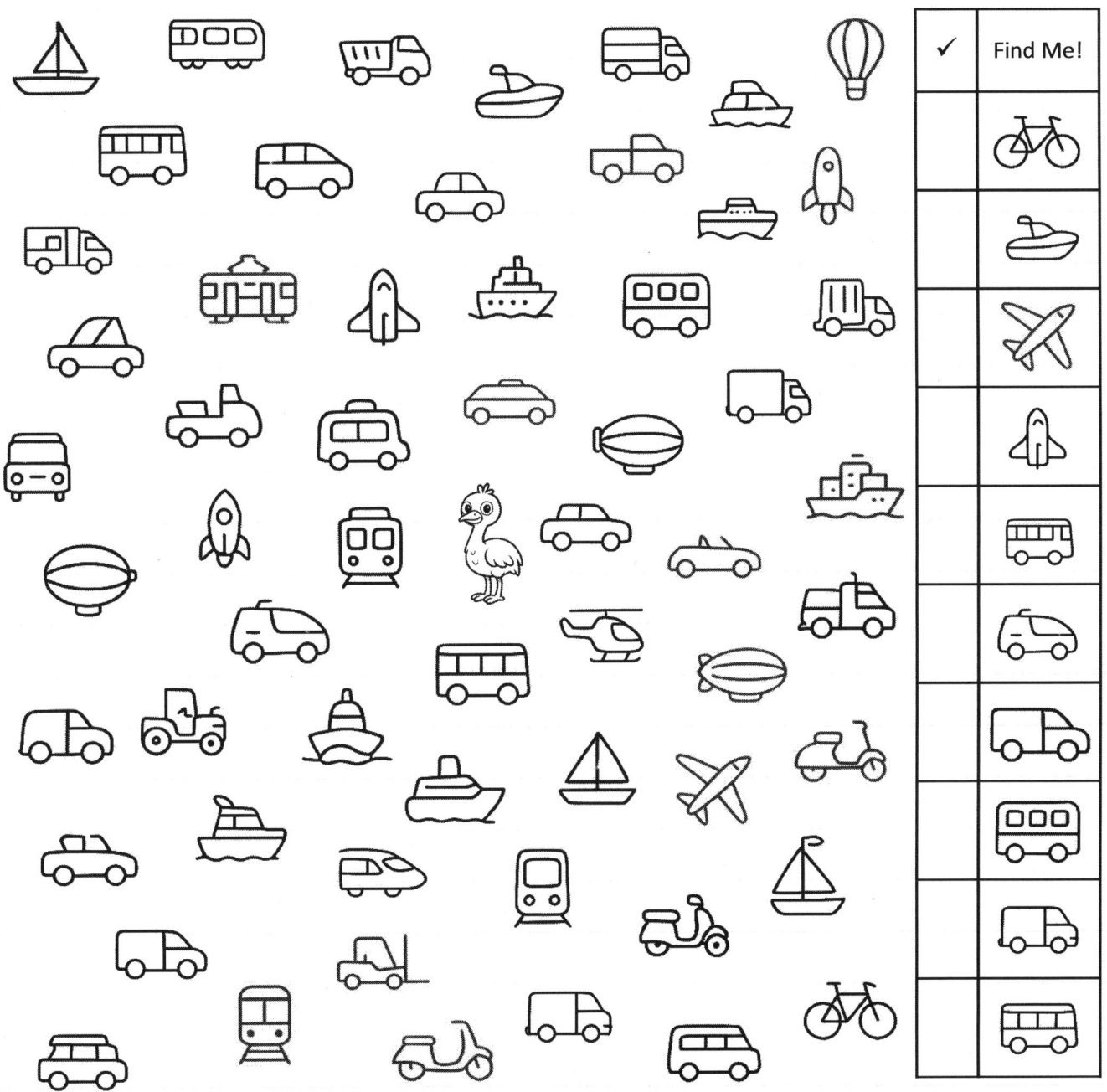

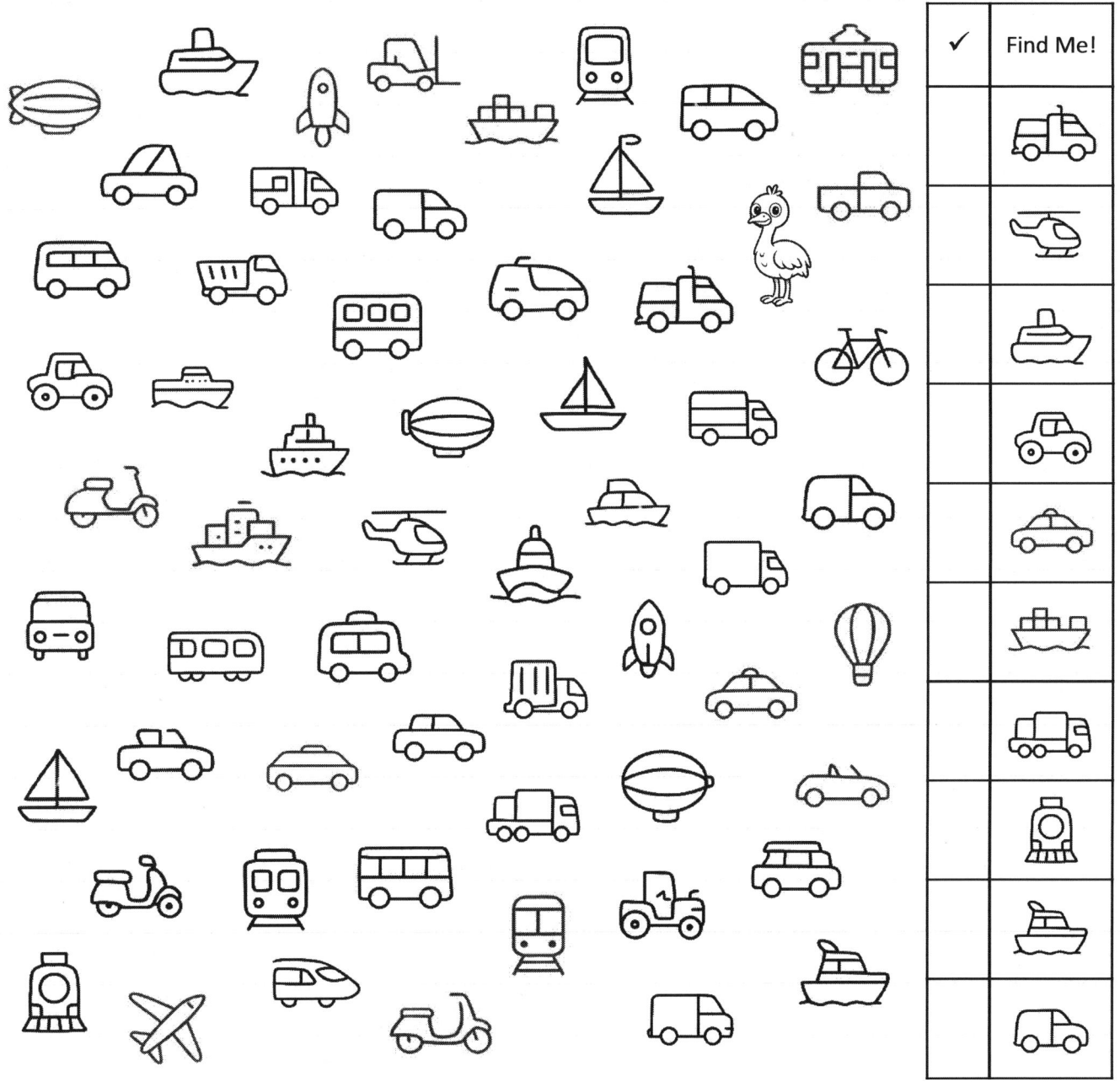

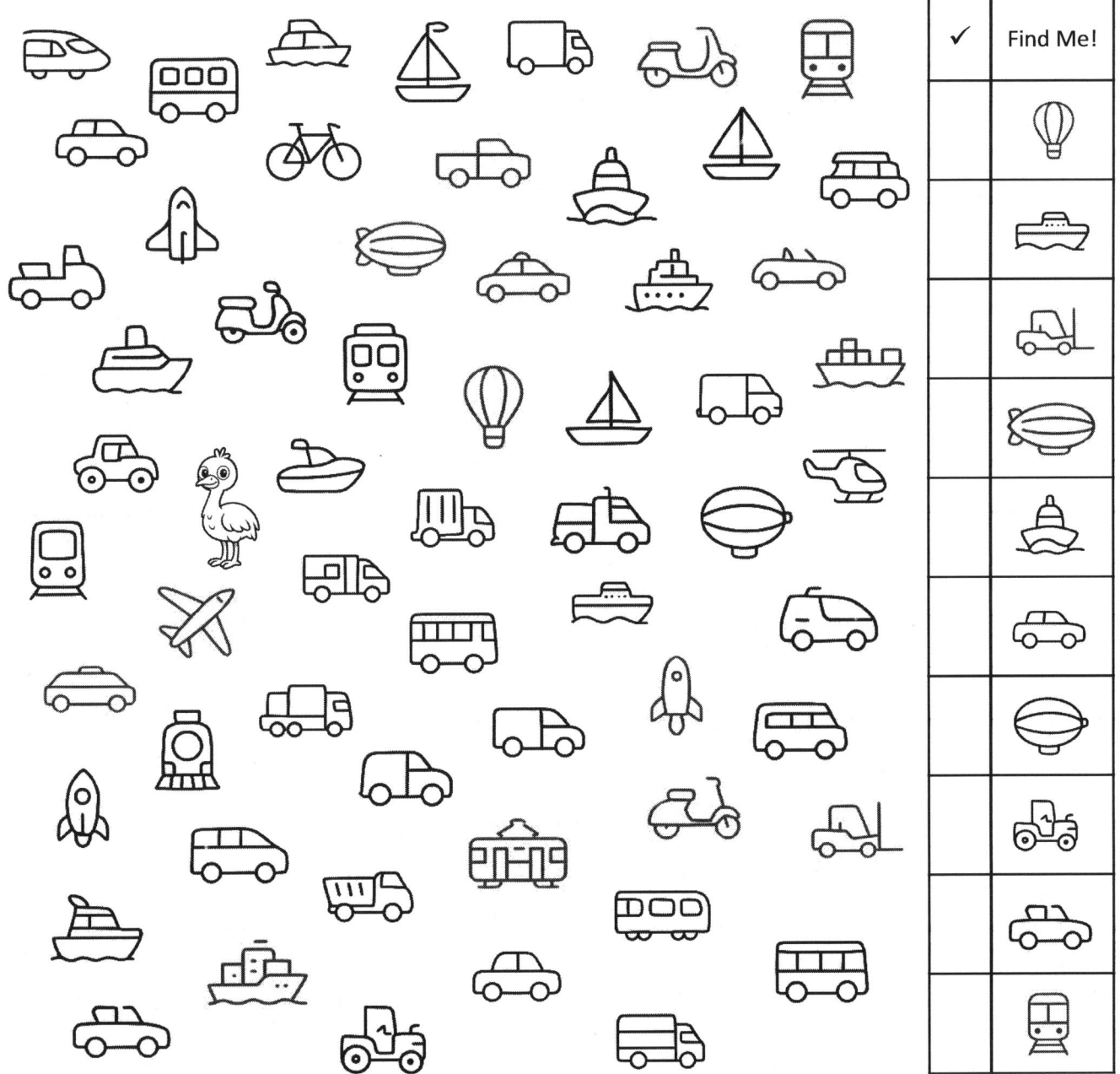

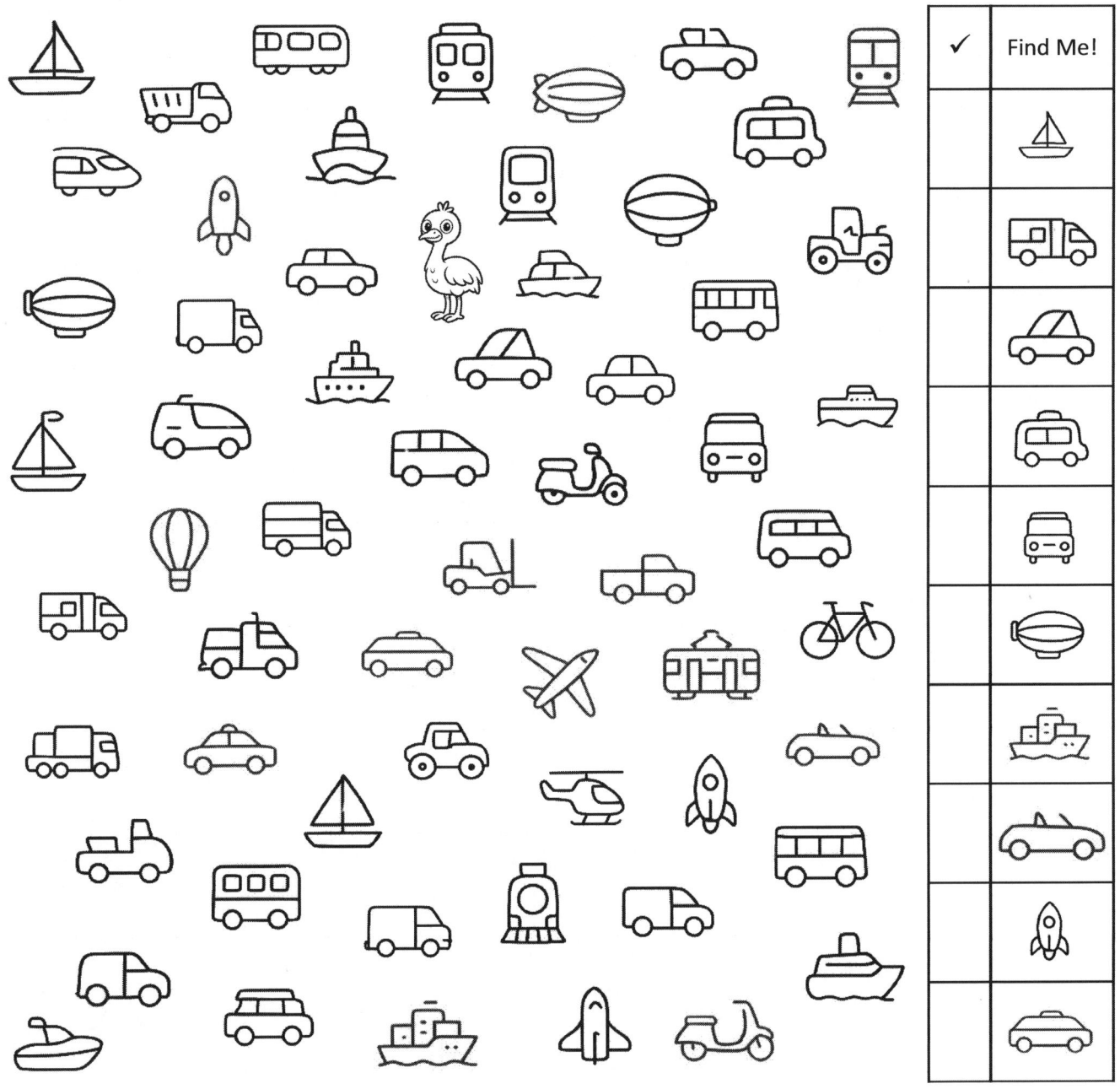

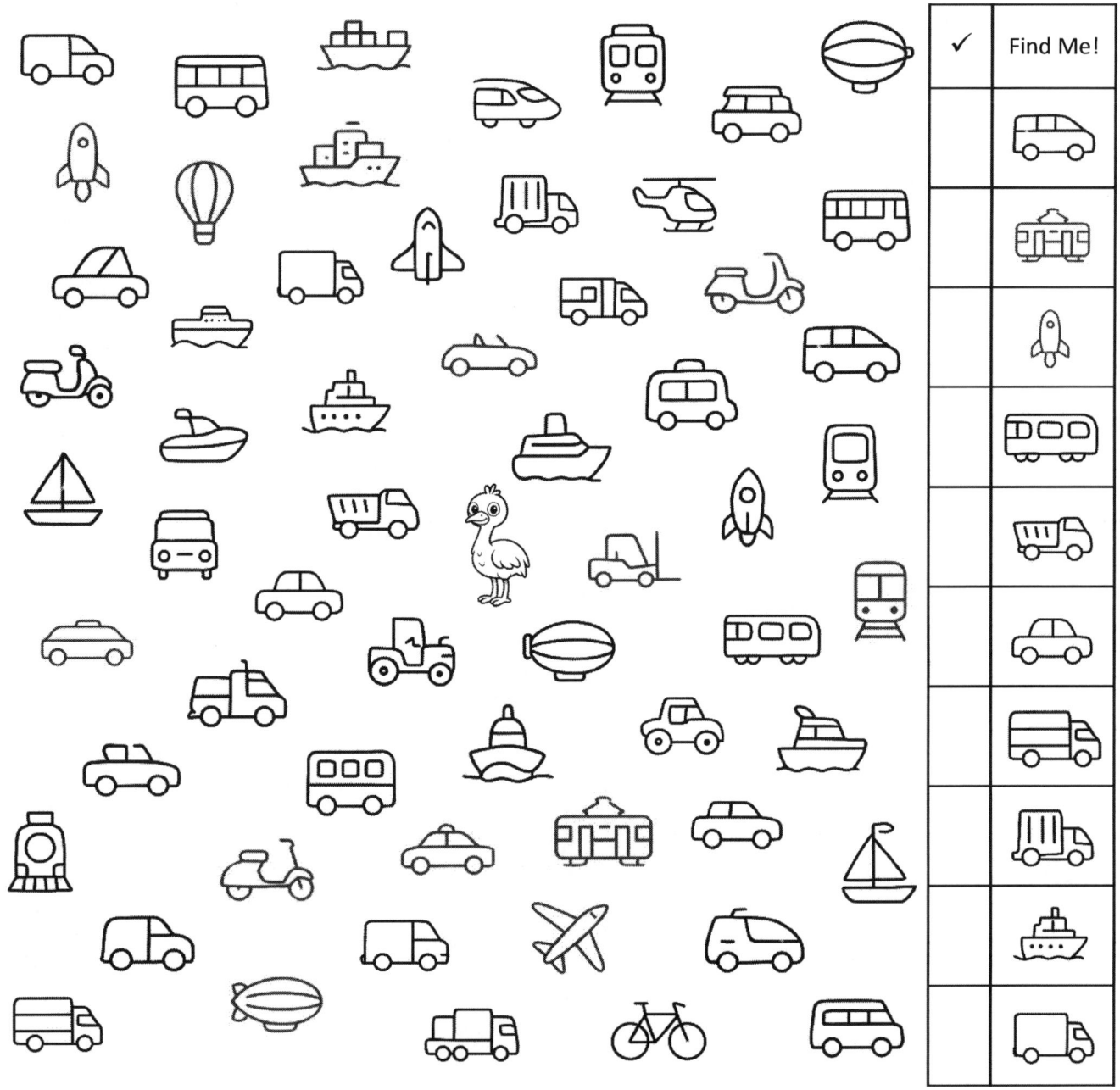

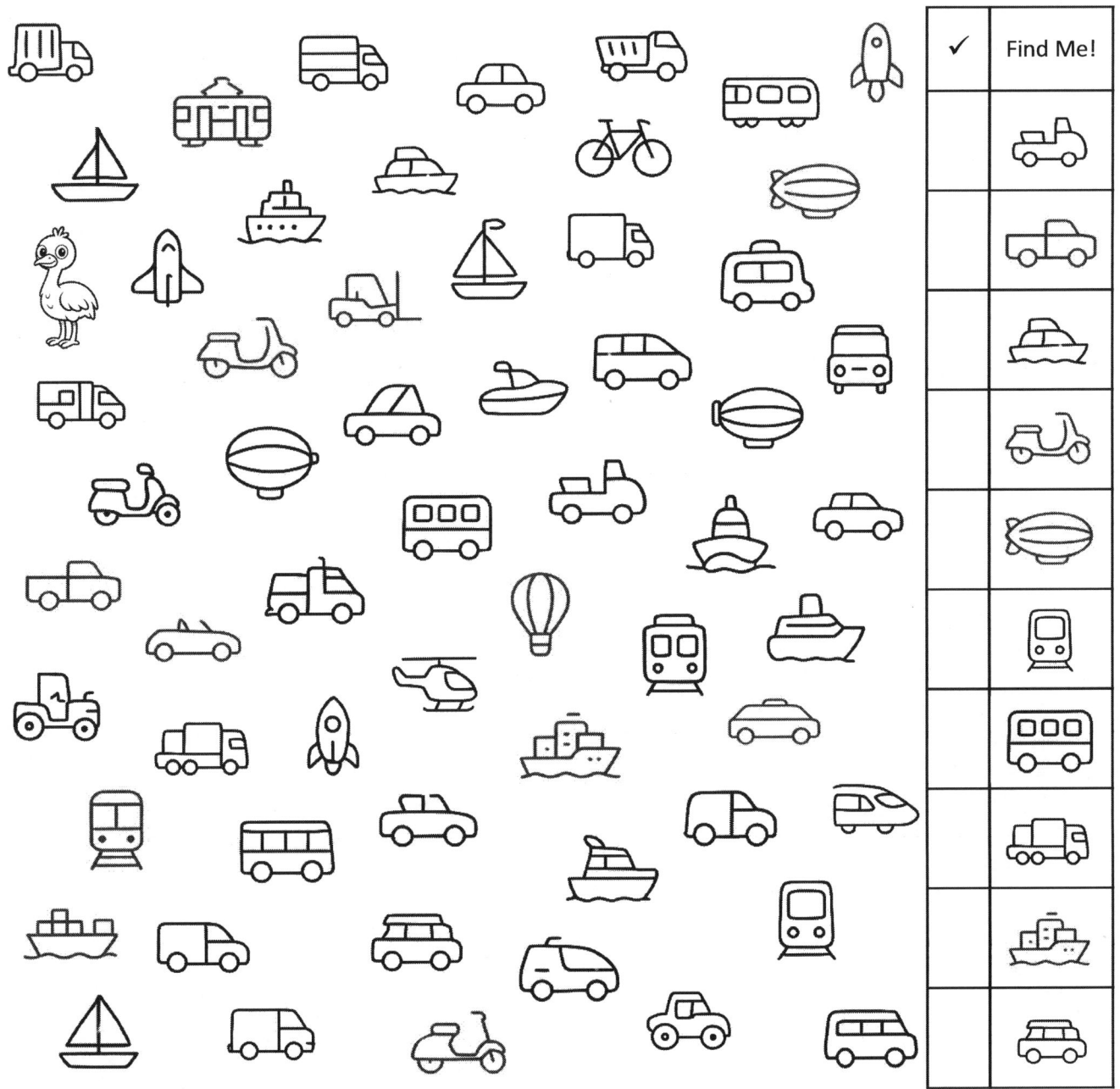

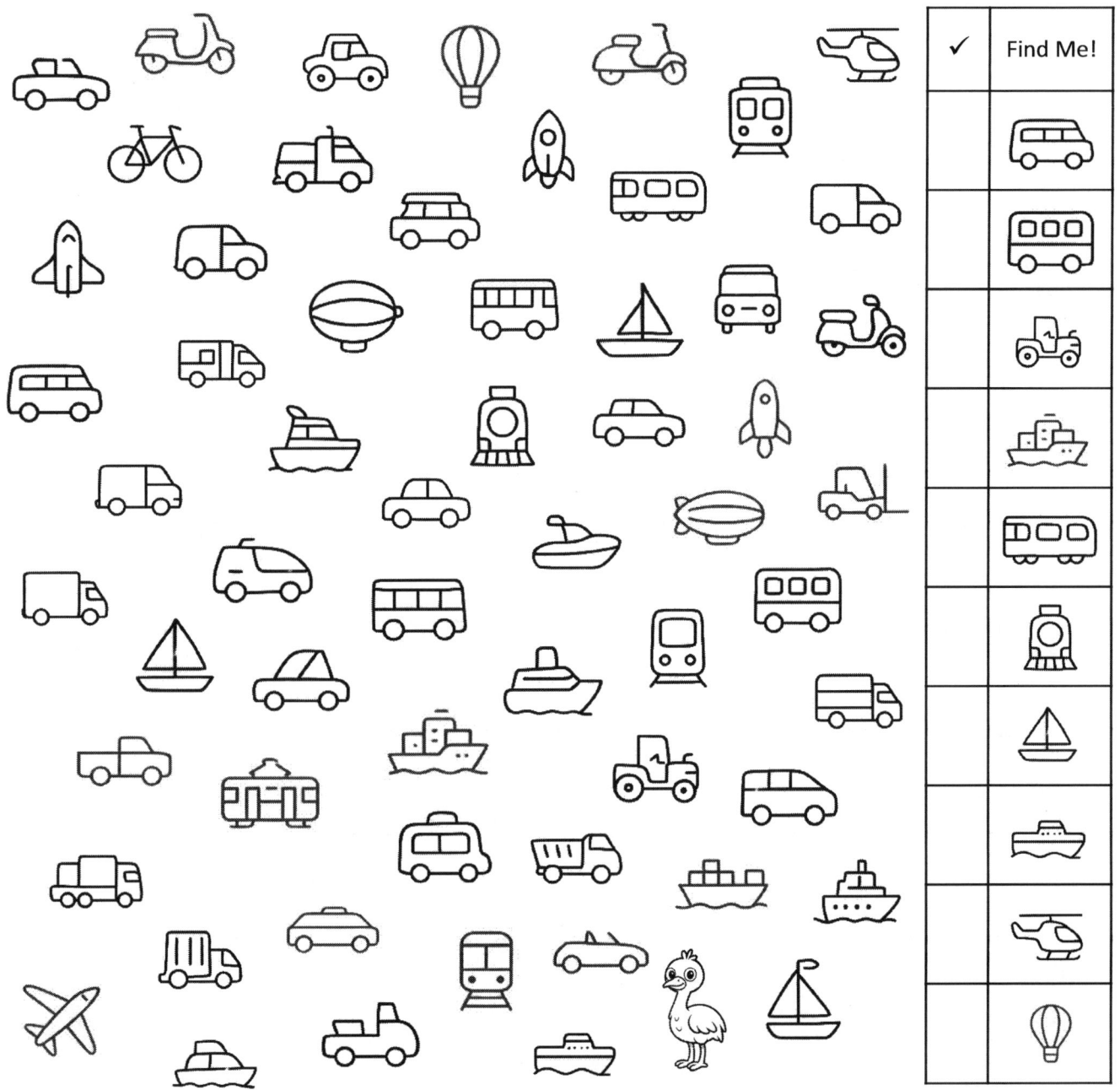

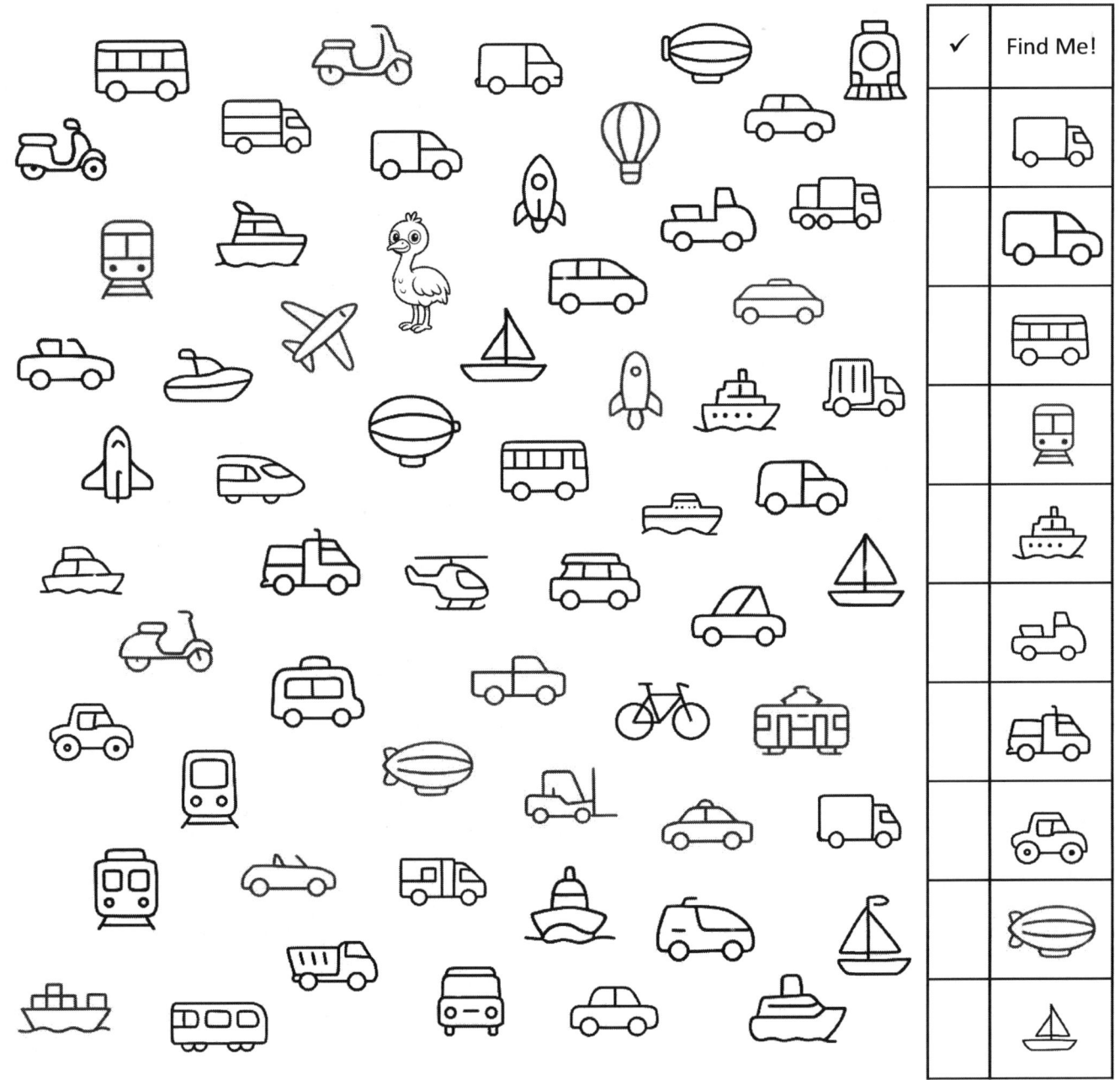

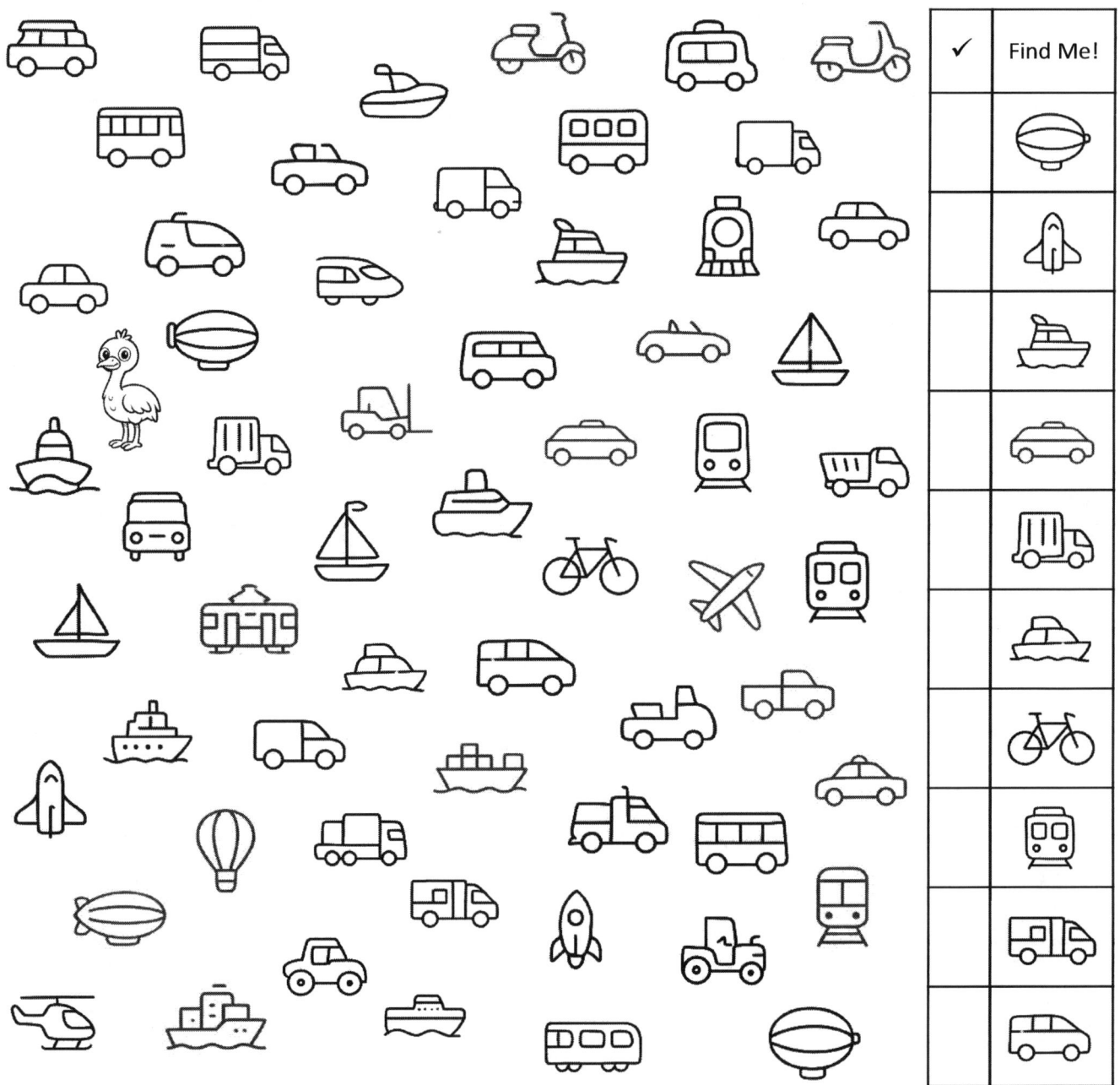

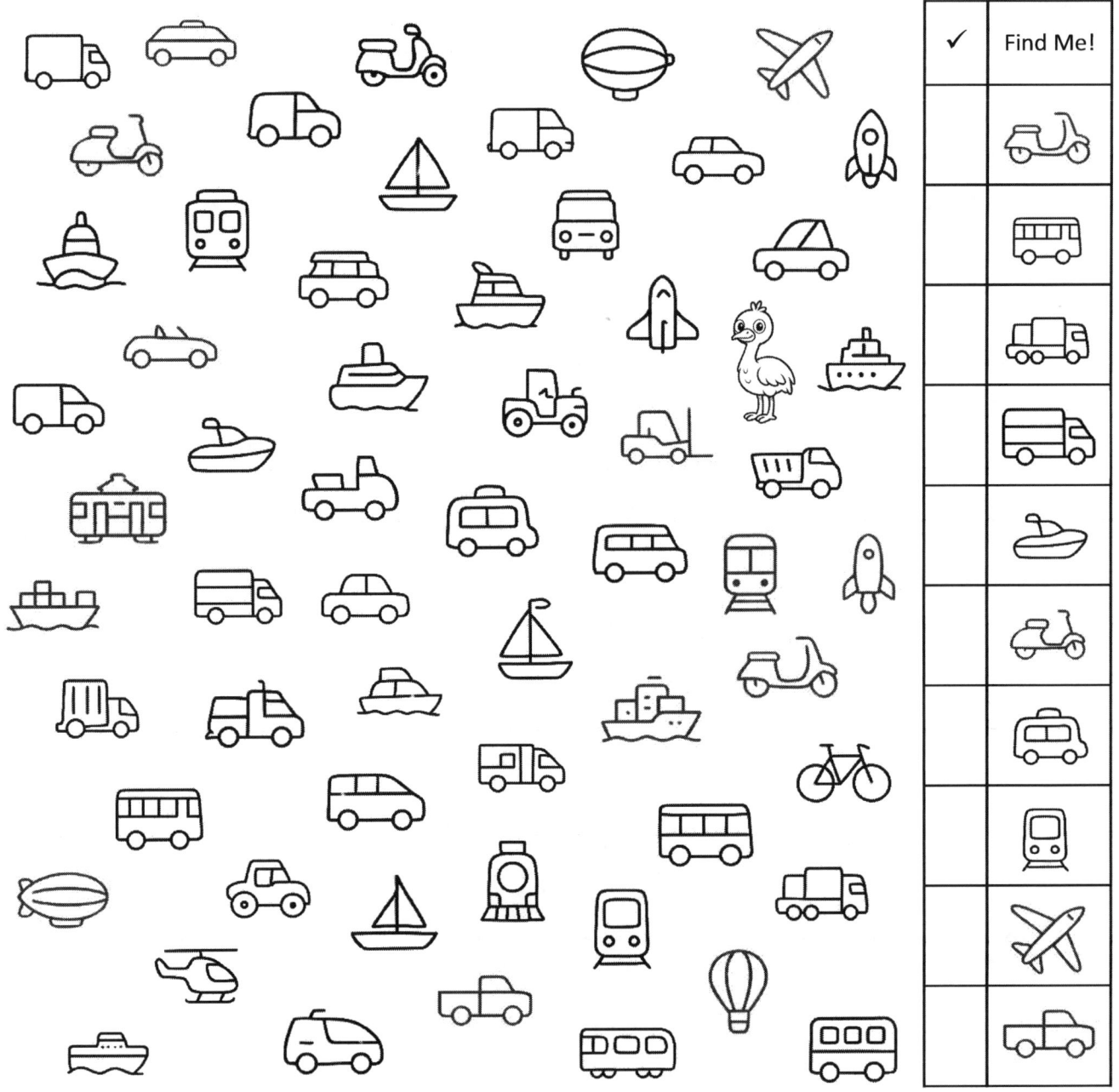

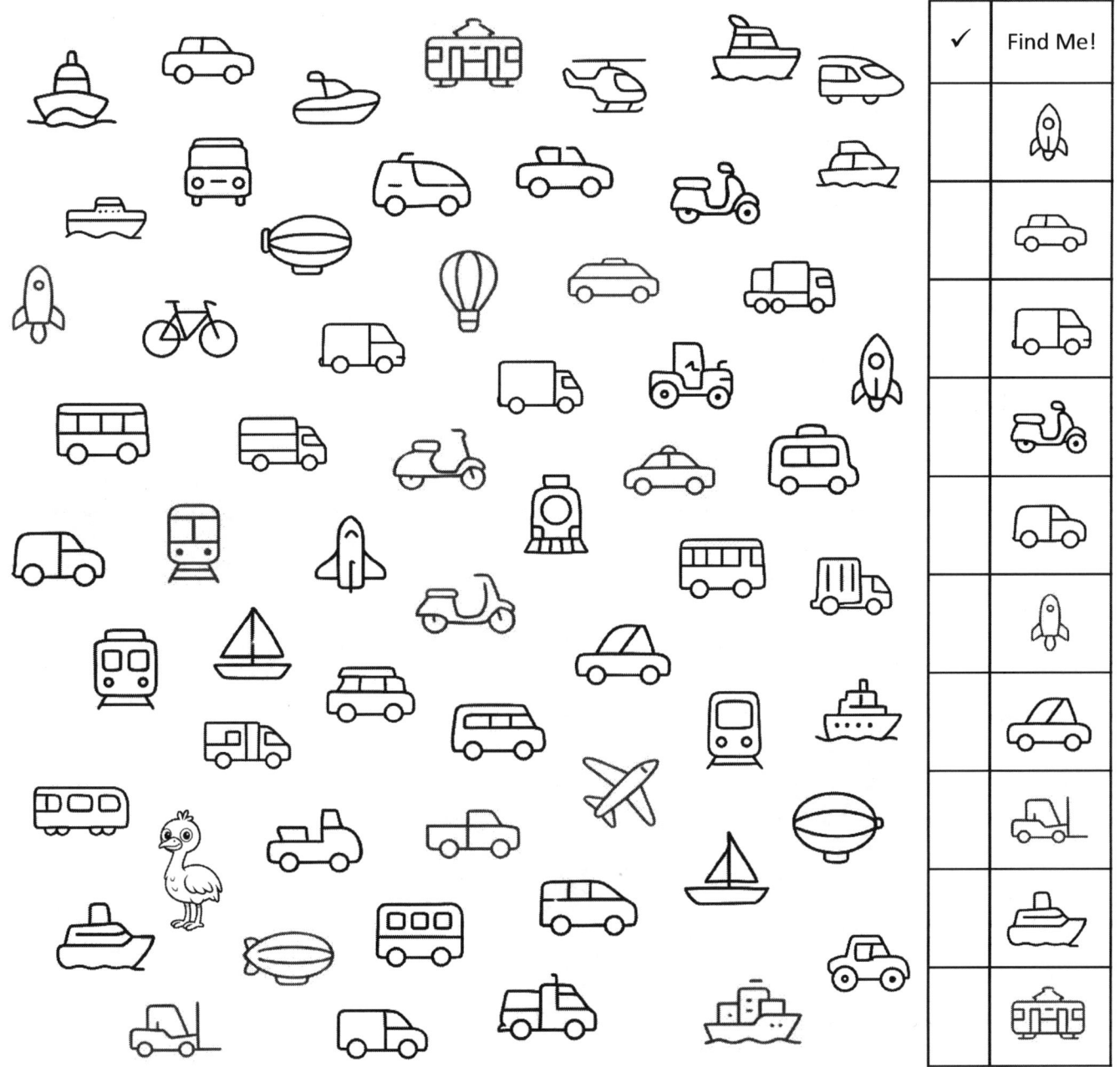

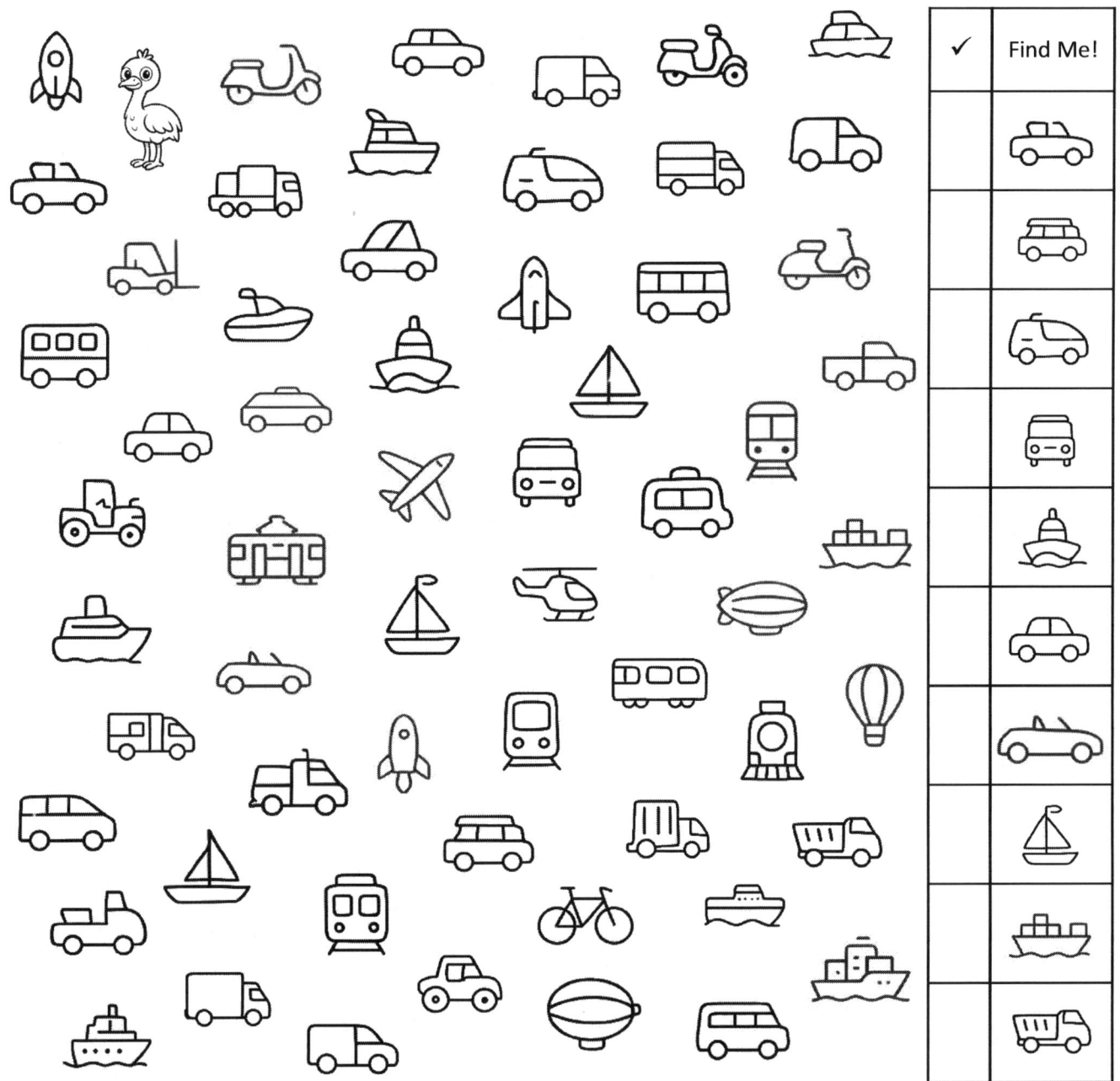

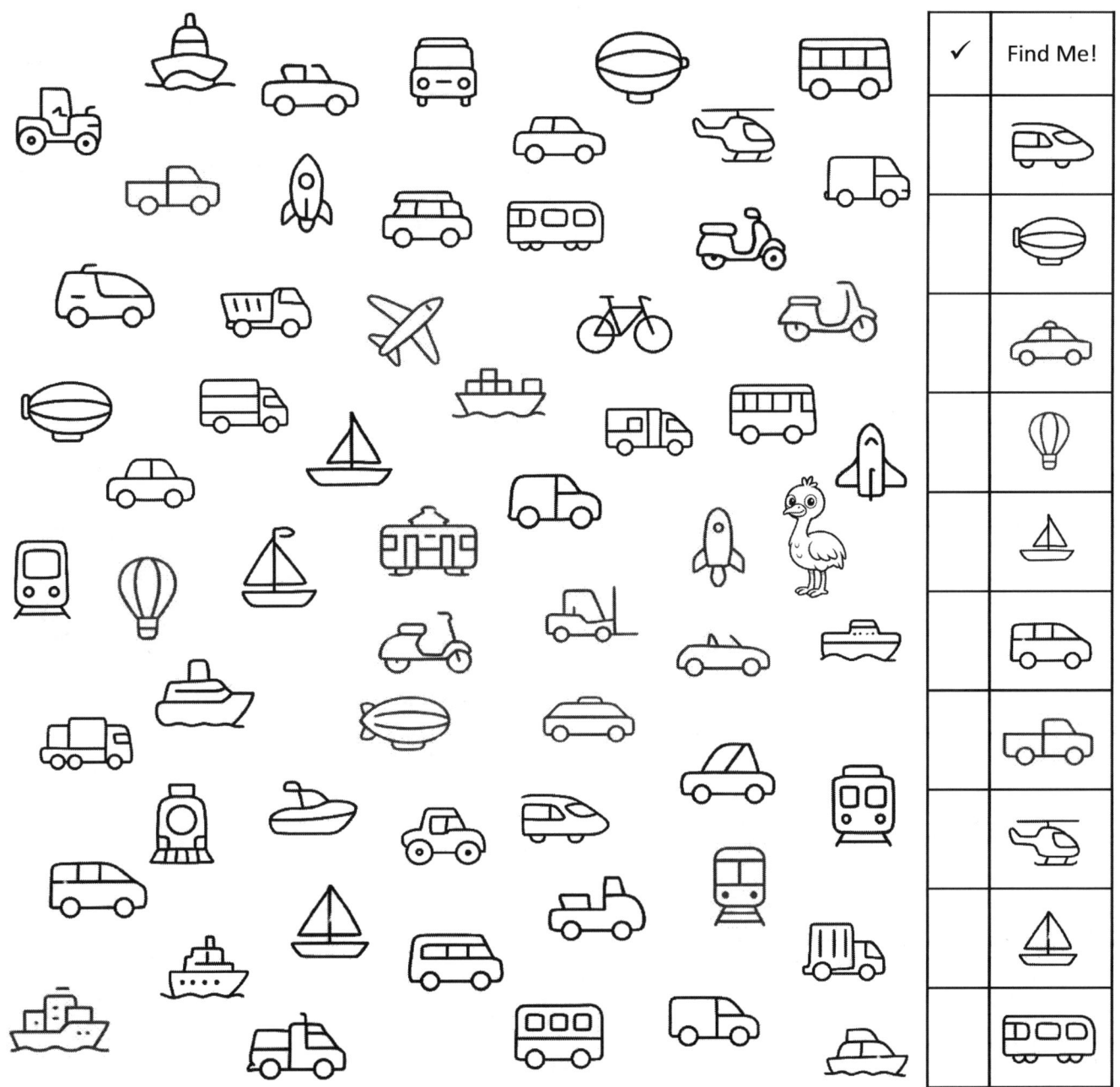

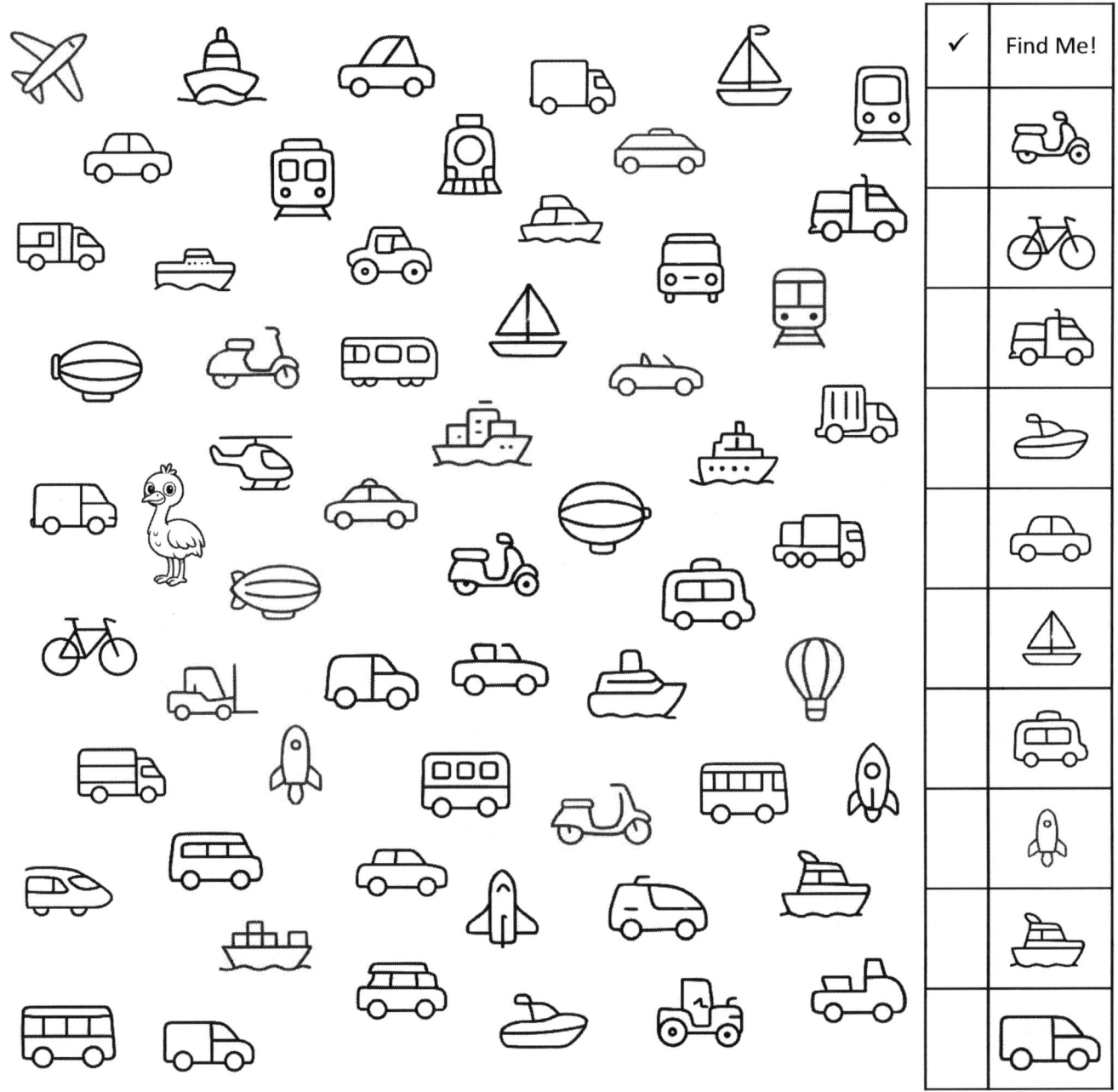

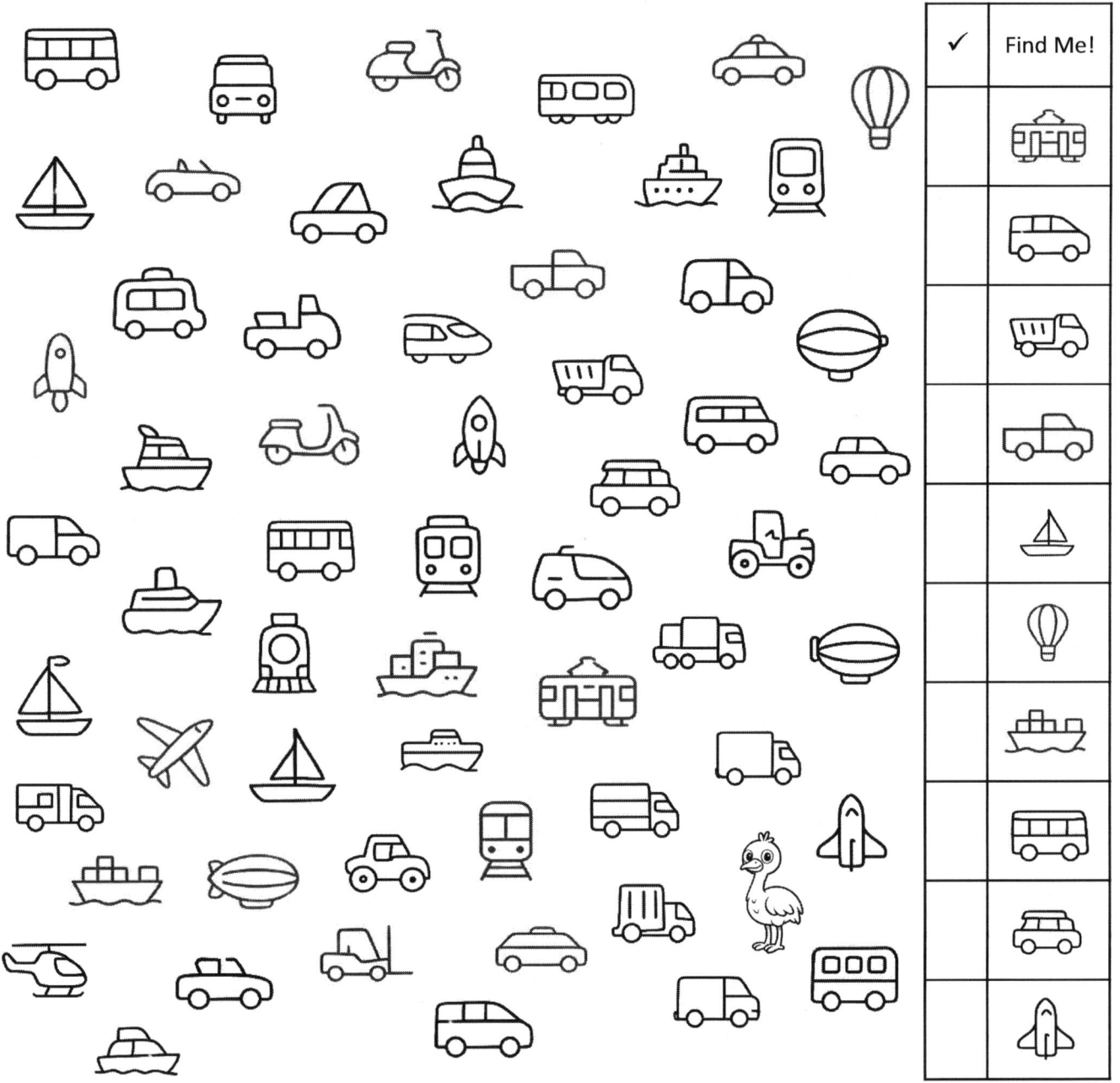

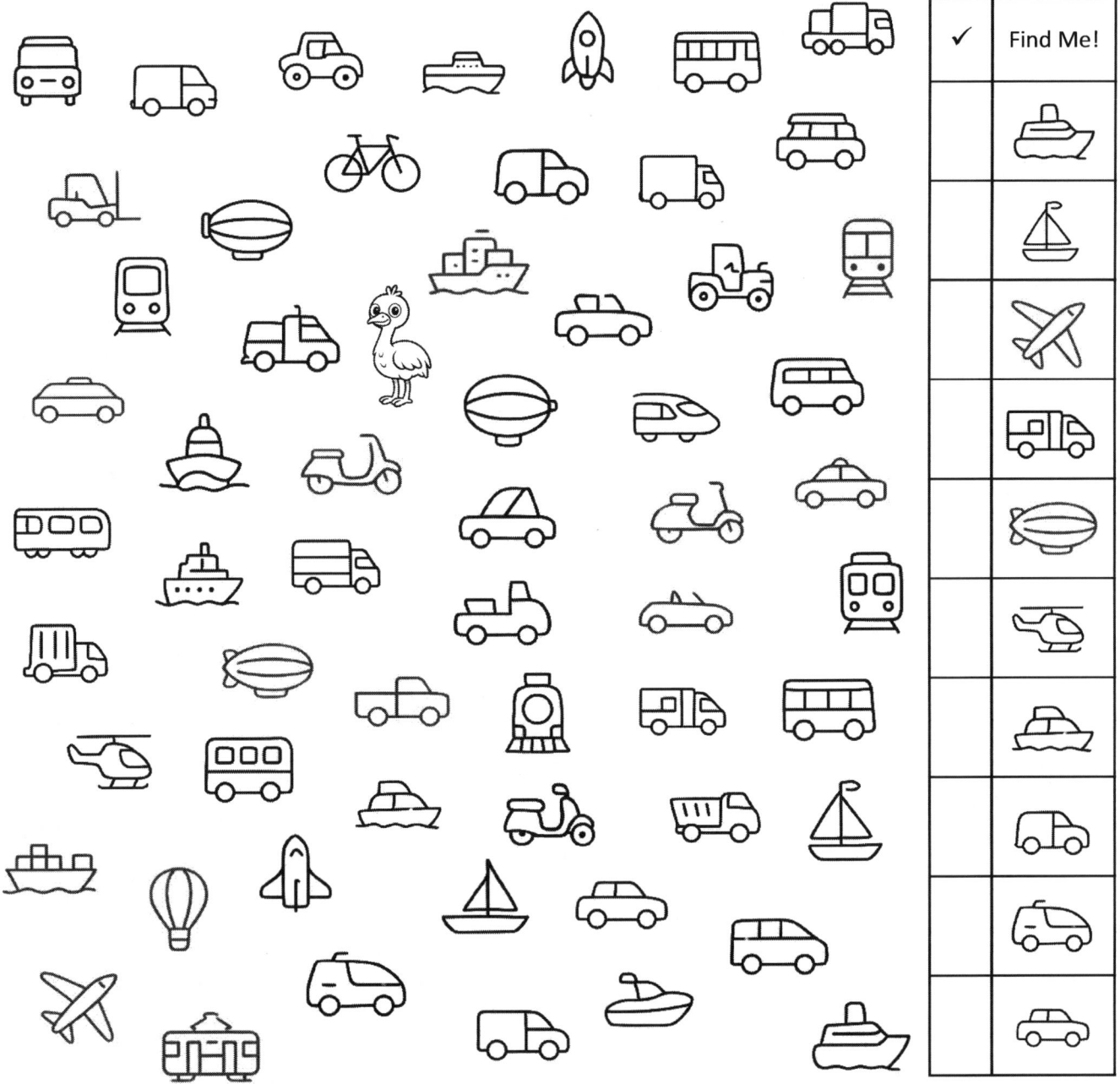

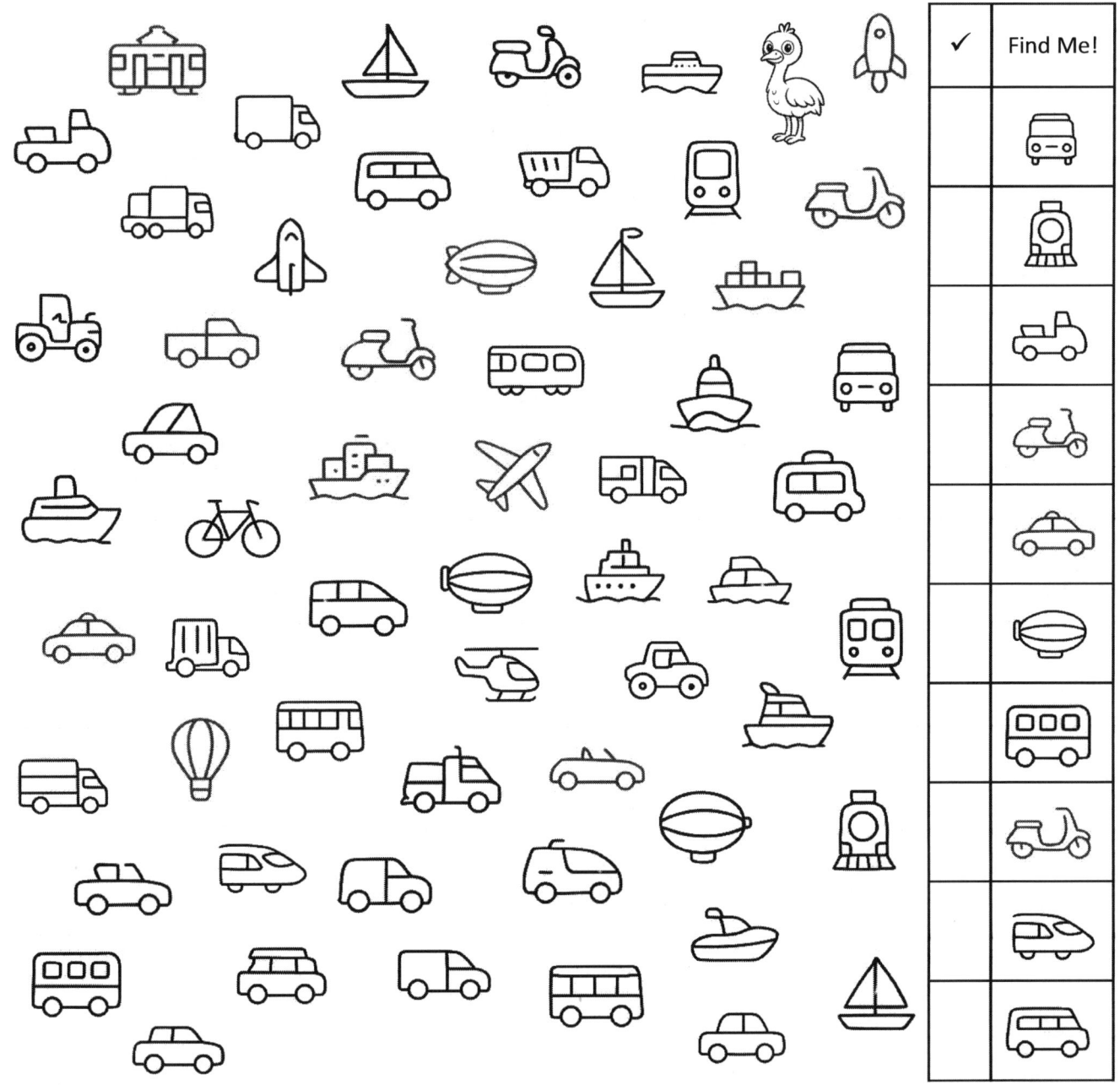

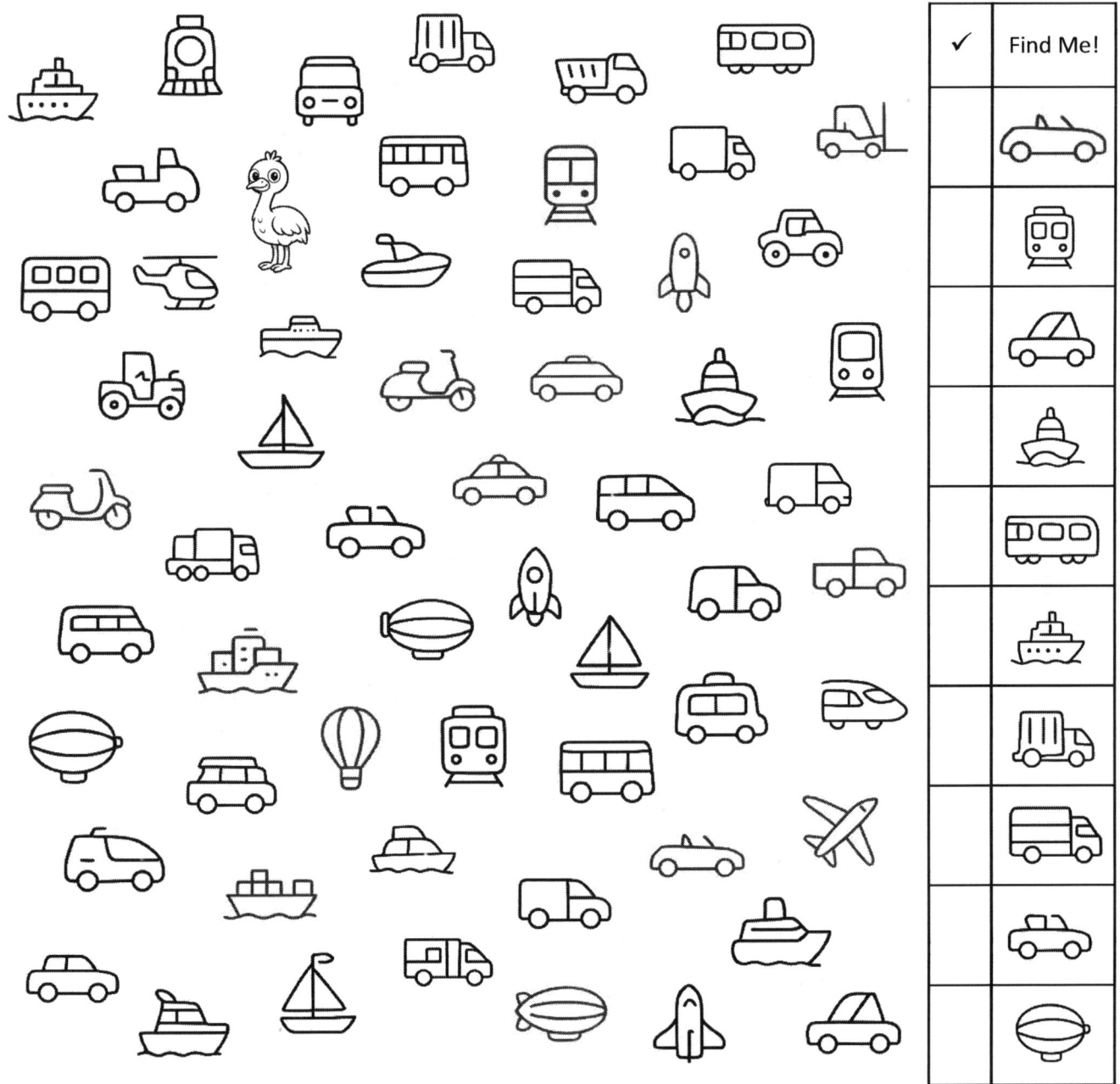

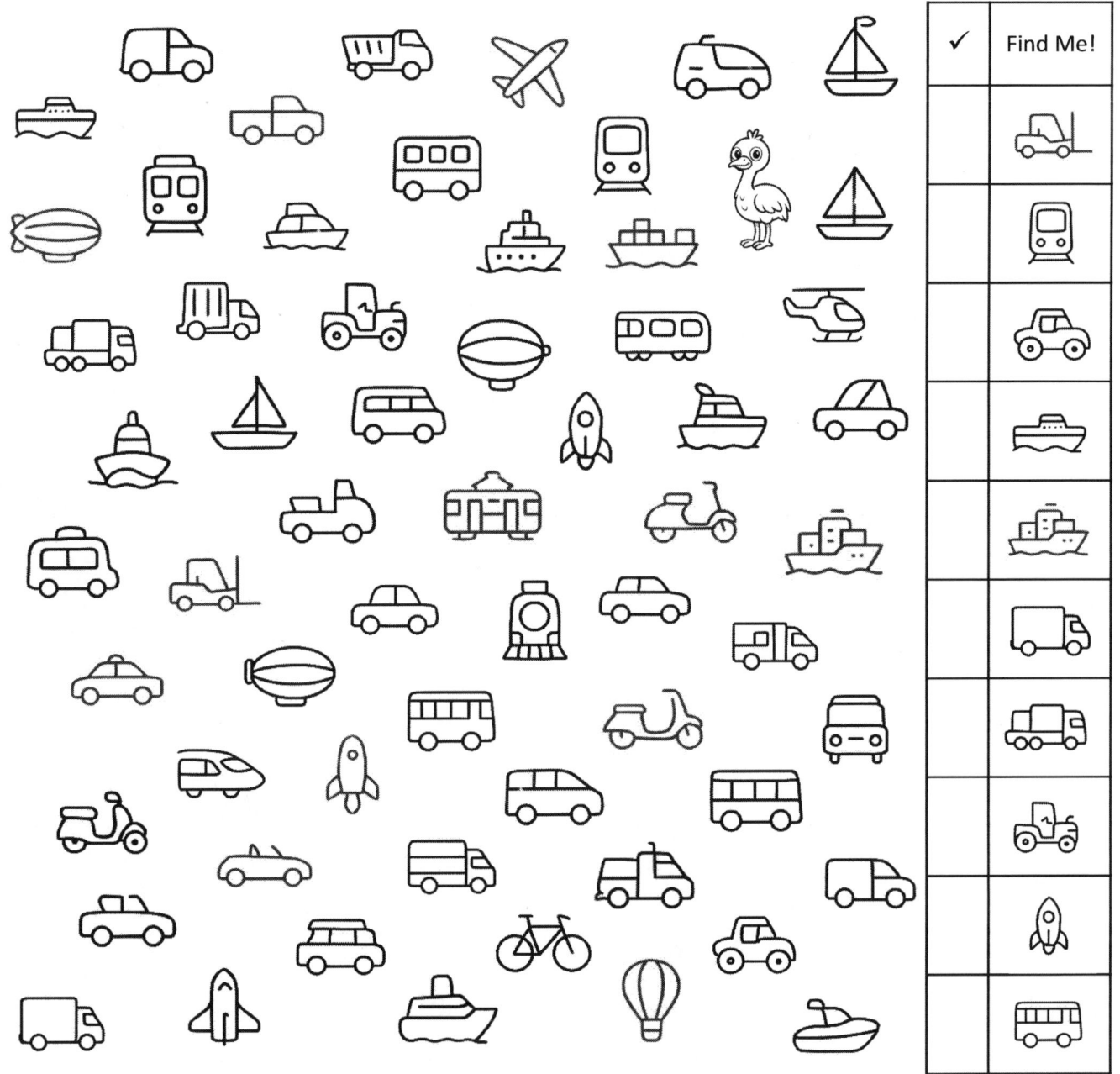

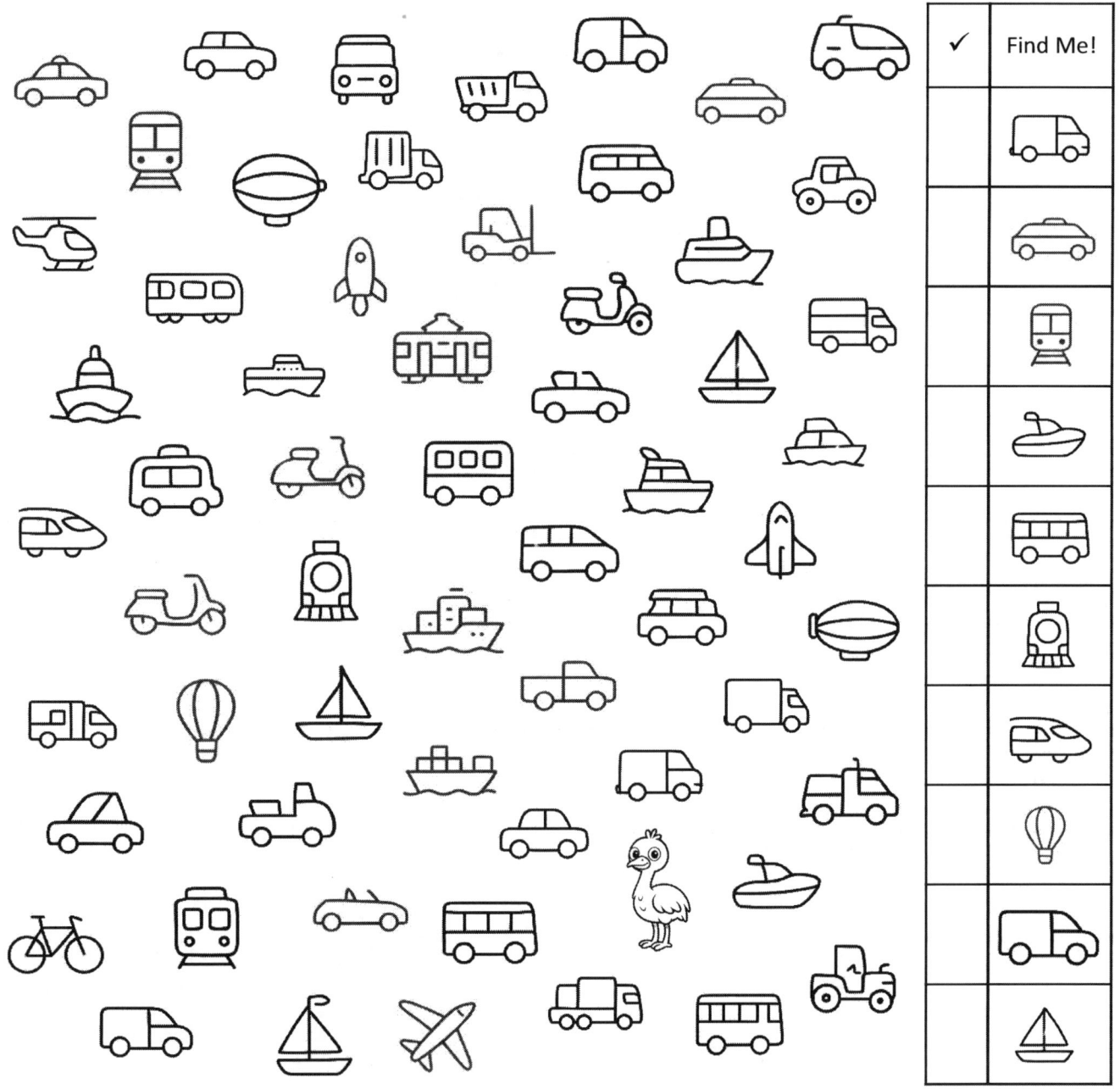

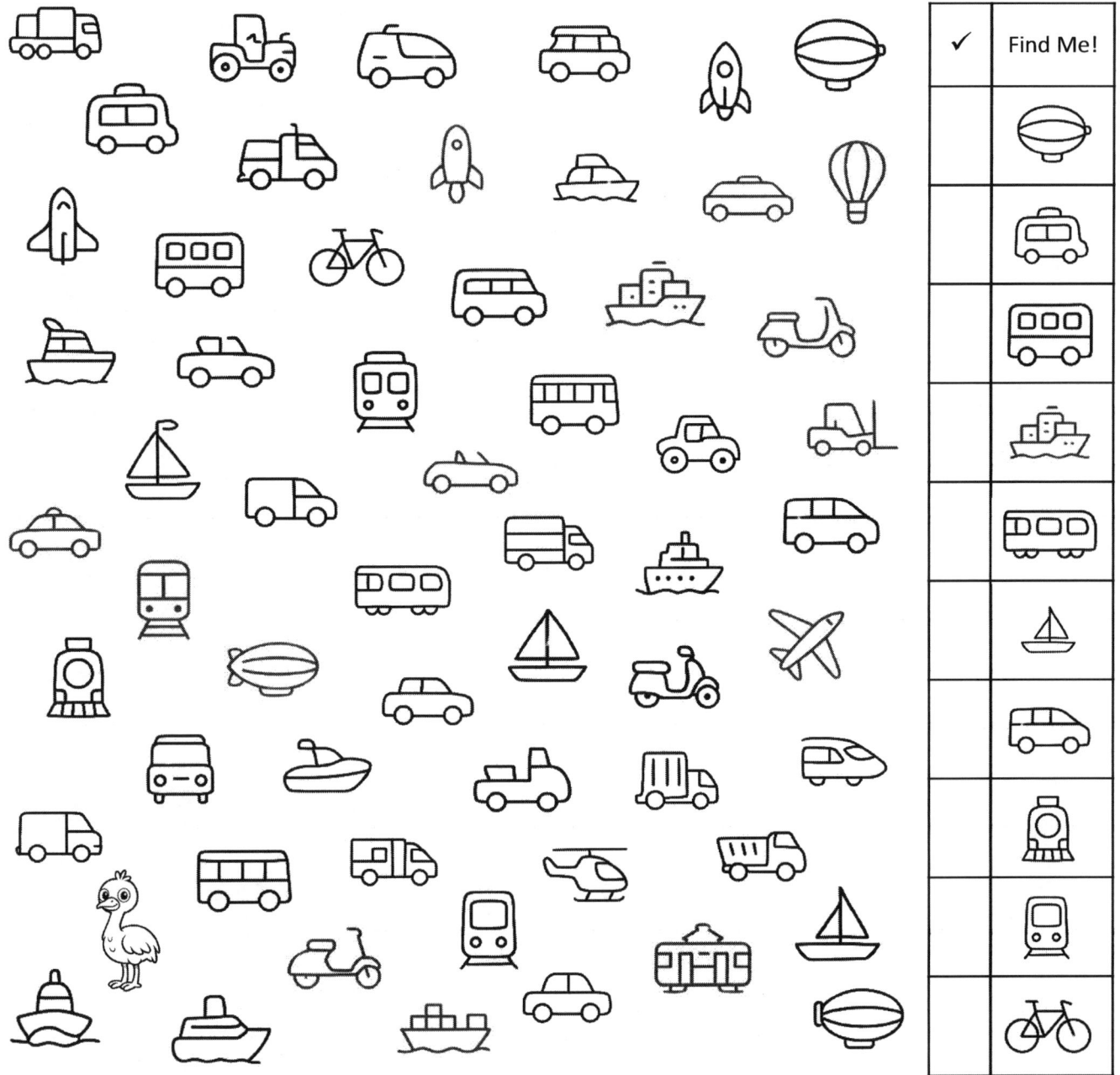

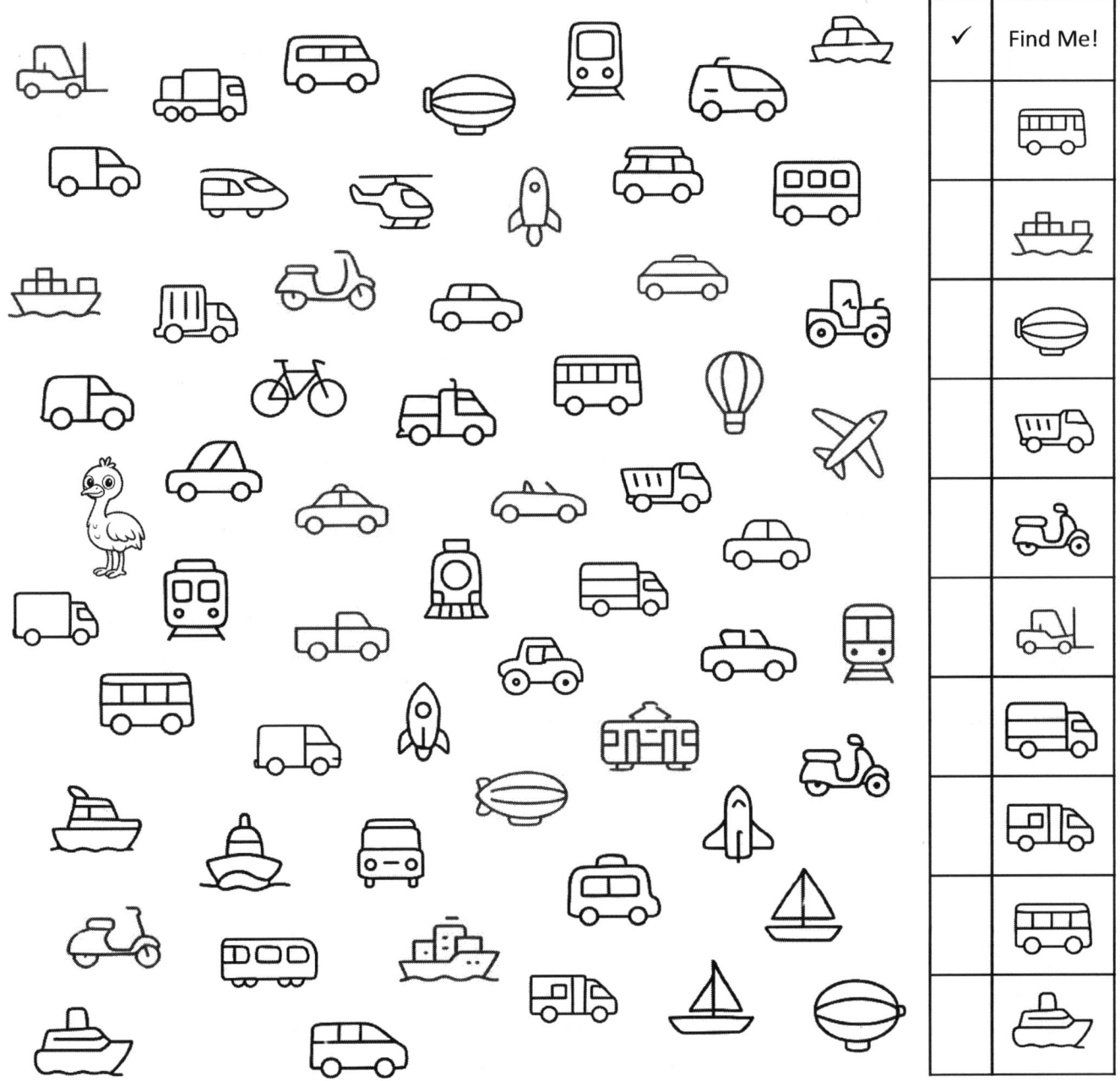

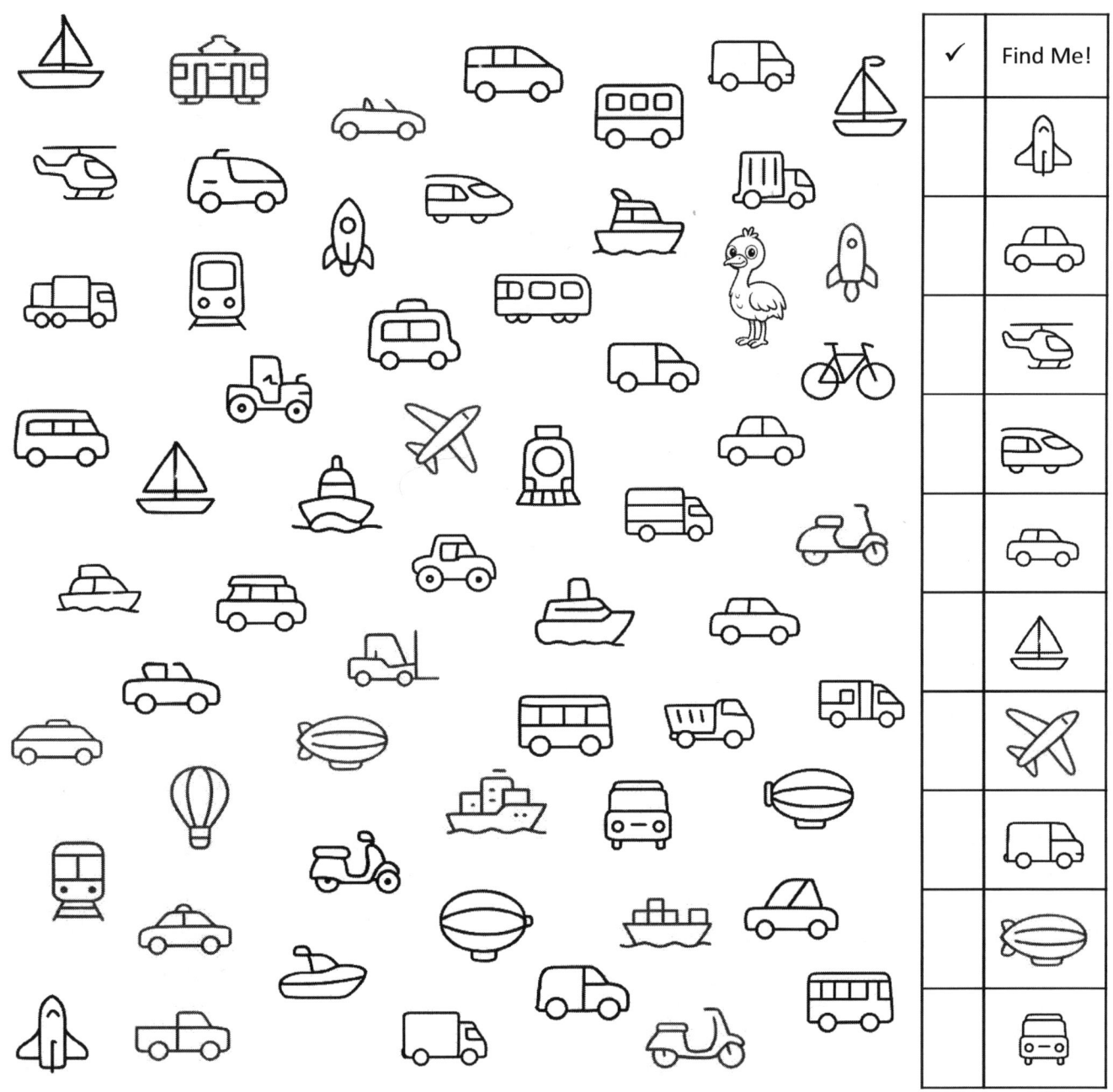

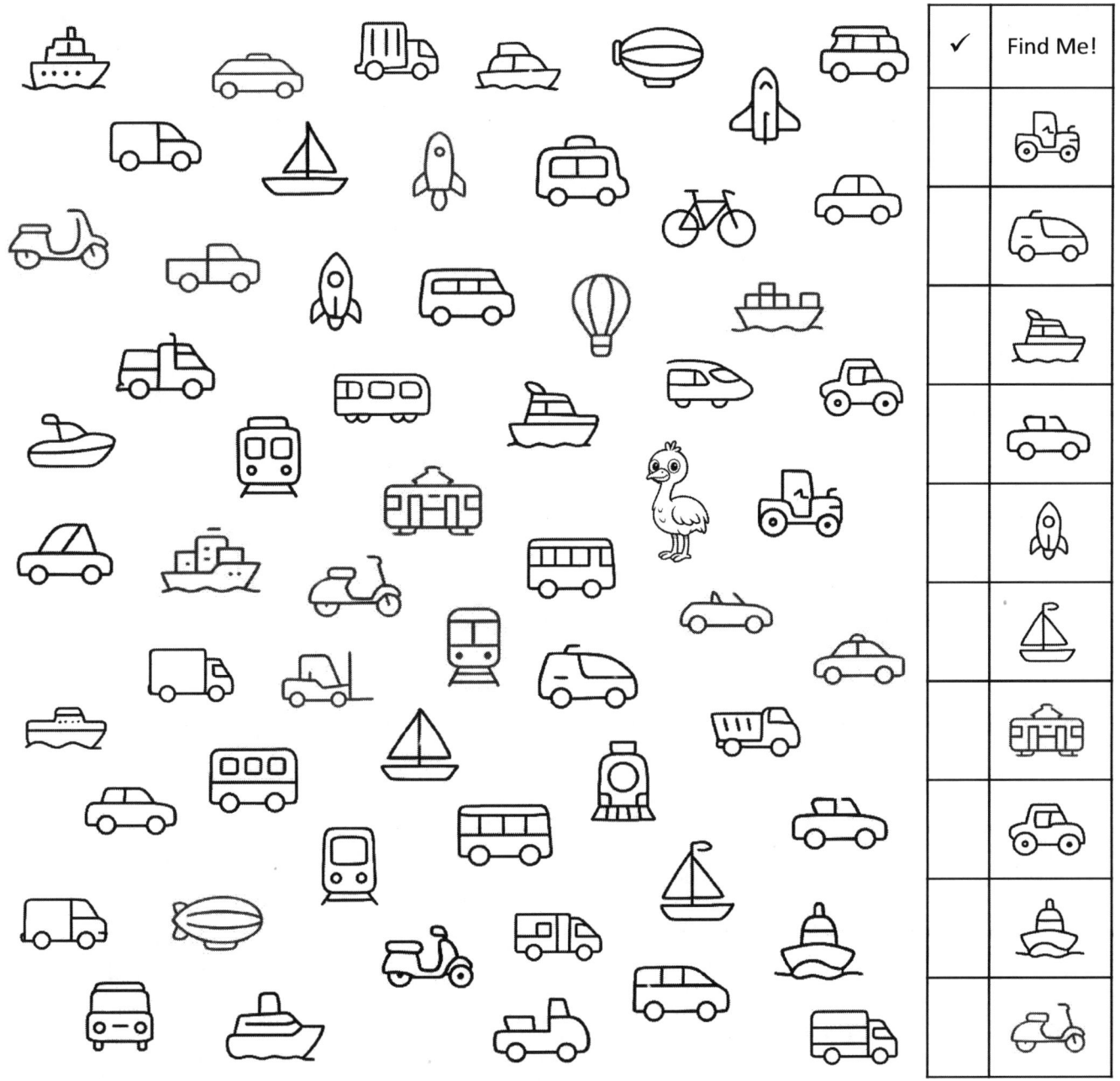

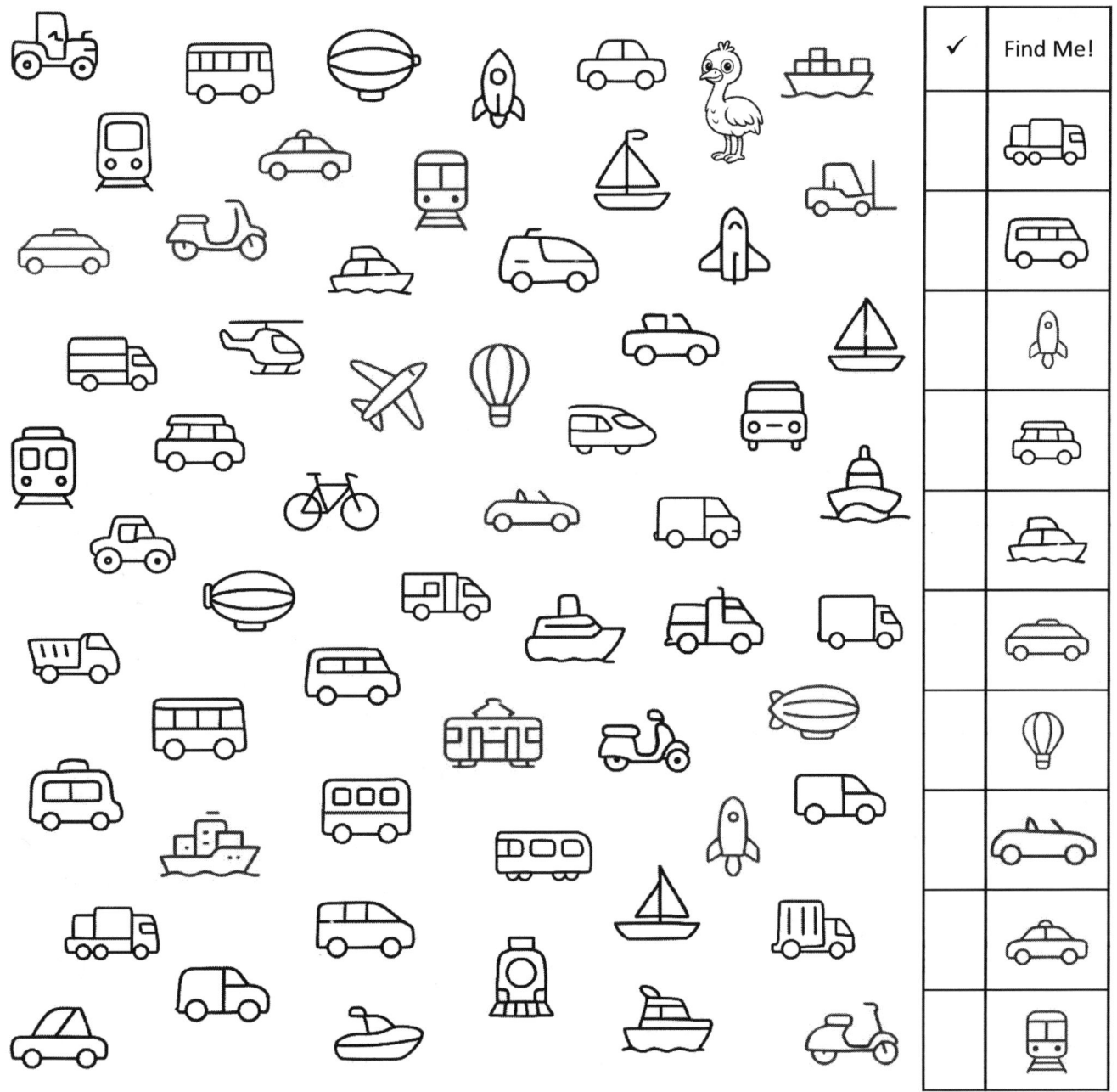

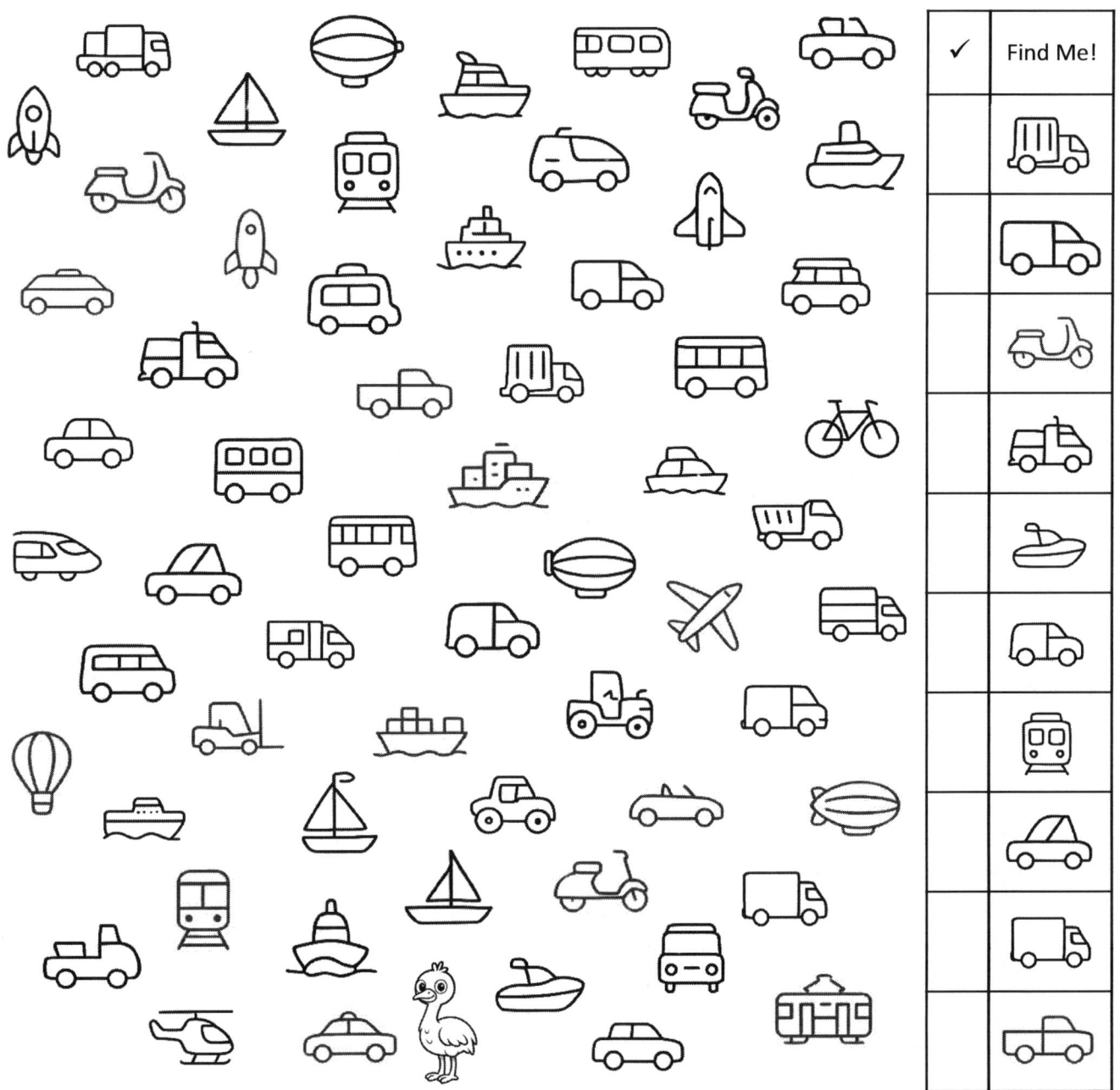

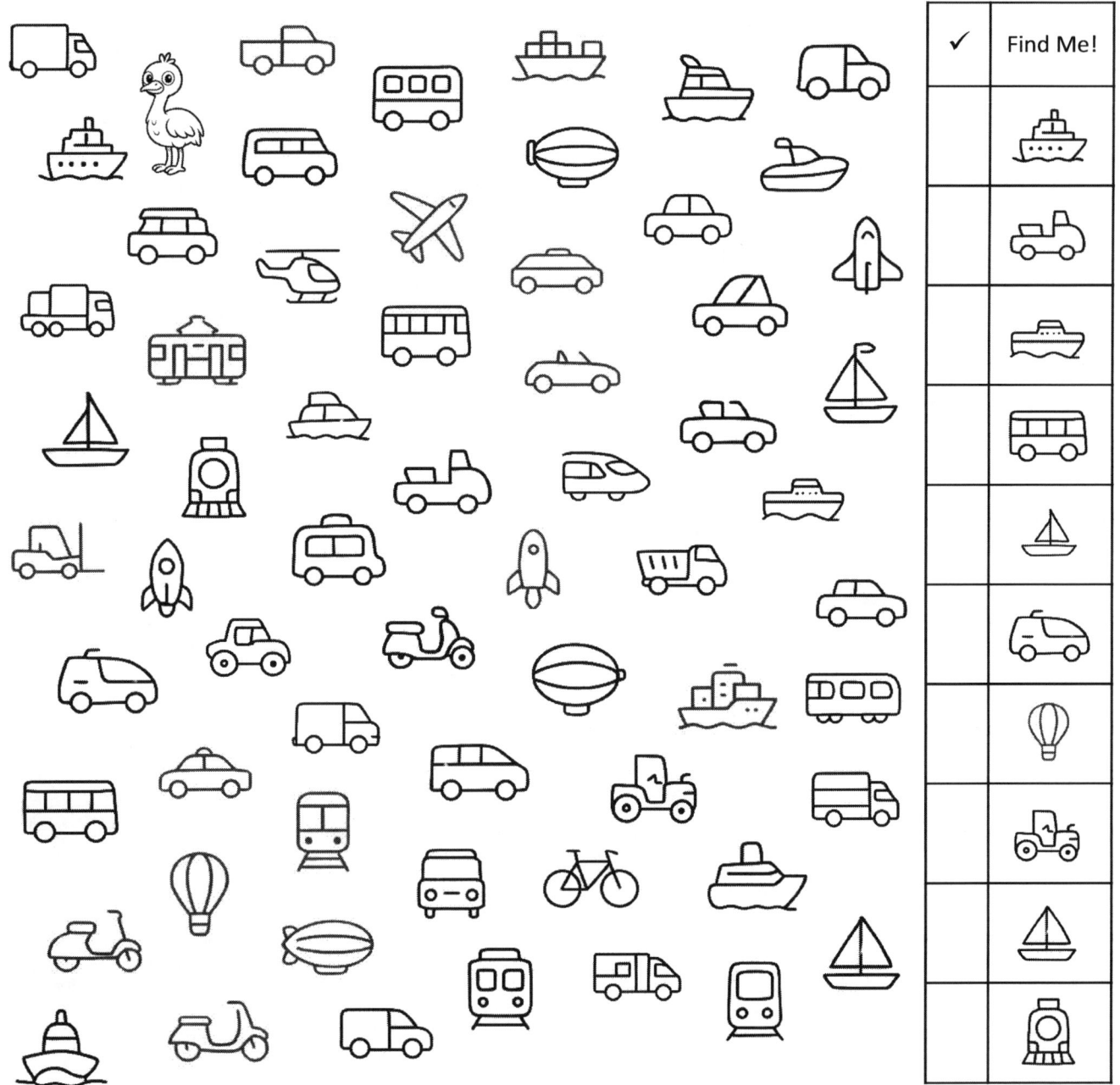

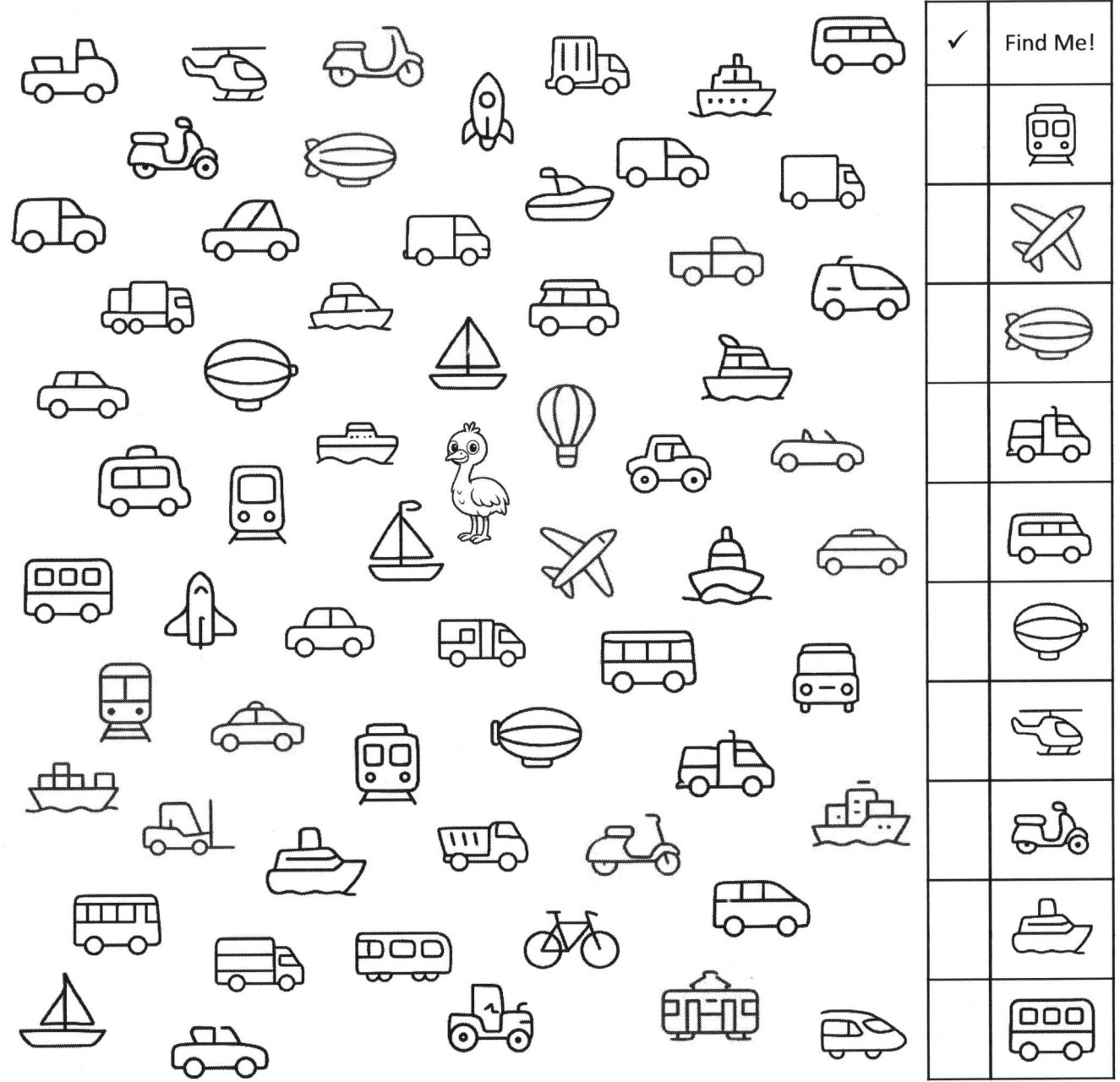

Printed in Dunstable, United Kingdom